AF576514

Memories of Home

William R. Smith

ISBN 0-7414-3953-0

Published by:

1094 New DeHaven Street, Suite 100
West Conshohocken, PA 19428-2713
Info@buybooksontheweb.com
www.buybooksontheweb.com
Toll-free (877) BUY BOOK
Local Phone (610) 941-9999
Fax (610) 941-9959

Printed in the United States of America

Printed on Recycled Paper

Published January 2008

Table of Contents

Acknowledgments

First of all I am most grateful to my spouse for accompanying me on my journeys to take photographs of places that I wanted to include in this book and for offering encouragement to complete the task once it was begun.

Secondly, I owe a great deal of gratitude to my parents for having provided me with a childhood that, upon reflection, gave me the tools needed to live a fruitful and satisfying life – experiences that I can fondly remember many, many years later. I would acknowledge, also, my four siblings whose lives continue to be an inspiration to me. I would be remiss, if I did not acknowledge a former neighbor of long ago and friend, Julian Shanholtz, who shared his memory with me of the murder of Henry Lee about which I write. I am indebted to Nadine Fox for allowing me to use a picture of her home. It is now the location of The Buck Valley Ranch – at one time the home of an aunt and uncle and boyhood best friend, Homer Fischer, all provide me with many pleasant memories. And those school mates of many years ago –Betty Smith and her brothers, Wayne, Grant, and Don; Marvin Oakman, probably my best friend in high school, the Stahle Brothers, Tom, Jim and Gene – there were many more unnamed contemporary childhood friends to whom I am greatly indebted. Lastly, I express my gratitude to grandparents, great uncles and great aunts, uncles and aunts, cousins and contemporaries of my parents who provided me with experiences that had a very lasting influence on my life.

And, contemporaneously I am grateful to my friend, Dr. Harry Bobonich, a former teaching colleague, whose conversations over coffee encouraged me to put into writing those experiences that I had growing up in small, very rural farming community in Pennsylvania during the late 1930's and early 1940's.

Memories of Home

Introduction

In 1940 Thomas Wolfe's novel, *You Can't Go Home Again,* was published posthumously. The character in Wolfe's novel could not go home again – everything had changed for him. And, unfortunately, nothing has changed since then; we still cannot return to the home of our childhood. Yes, the house may still be standing as are many of the land marks that we associate with our concept of home, – but, so many of the elements and components, taken in the aggregate, that made a "locale" home are missing – parents, grandparents, siblings, other specific people, familiar family names, customs, dirt roads, general stores, antiquated billboards and road signs, customs, traditions, mores—even our own frame of mind are missing. All are replaced now by different family names, supermarkets with large paved parking areas, hard surfaced roads, electronically lighted billboards and other evidences of modernity that were not there fifty or sixty years ago – and our life experiences have so modified our inner world that we can never see our "old" home in the same context as we once did.

However, memory has a way of ignoring or blocking out many of these changes that inevitably occur with the passage of time. And, upon reflection, many of the scenes, events, both tragic and joyful, and people we knew in another era and place are resurrected, and once again, we can go home again – if only in memory!

During my lifetime I have lived in several places that I called home. Prior to the age of six my home was in a house in Pittsburgh, Pennsylvania. As a seventeen year old when in the military I lived in barracks that I called home. As a college student, after marriage, we lived in a rented house in a small college town for a couple years, that was home. After graduation we lived for a short time in a mobile home in a mobile home park that was home. Later, we rented a house in a small town called Halifax, Pennsylvania, that was home. Employment took us to Harrisburg, Pennsylvania, where we built a house and lived there several years, that was home, and finally, we bought about five and a half acres of land just outside of Newburg, Pennsylvania and built a house. That has been home for thirty–six years. But the home I want to write about is where I spent approximately eleven years after my family left Pittsburgh, Pennsylvania and moved to a small farm in rural Fulton County, Pennsylvania. Our address at that time was Northcraft, Pennsylvania. My grandfather had a general store and post office, grandfather was the postmaster – on the map it was designated as a village about a mile from where we lived. After 1941, when the Northcraft Post Office was closed, our address, even though we didn't move, was changed to Amaranth, Pennsylvania.

Until a few years ago I made a number of visits back "home". Especially while my parents were living – and even after they passed away I still would visit my aunts and uncles who continued to live in the same homes in which they lived when I was a boy. When these relatives eventually passed away fewer and fewer trips were made by me to this familiar part of the county.

Chapter 1

A Trip Back

Out of a feeling of nostalgia, I suppose, one beautiful day in mid October 2006, my wife and I decided to make a return visit to the old stamping grounds. I checked out my cameras, decided on a route and started the drive. We would drive to Hancock, Maryland – have lunch in a restaurant that we remembered from high school days, and then travel west on Old Route 40. Route 40 was usually the route my parents took when we went to Hancock, Maryland to shop or see one of the doctors that practiced there. Plus, I had other memories of Route 40 that I could recall. Let me share a couple with you.

No Peach Pickers Needed

There was the time that my friend and neighbor, Robert Shanholtz, and I walked along route 40 west from an orchard on the west side of Hancock for a distance of about 15 miles! Early that morning we had ridden our bikes to a friend of Robert who was working on an orchard picking peaches. We decided we'd get a job also and work for a few weeks before school started. I was fifteen and Robert was a few month younger than I. So, we rode our bike for a distance of about five miles to where Robert's friend lived.

We had to wait a few minutes until he had finished his farm chores and then we got into his car and rode to the orchard with him. The orchard was just west of Hancock, Maryland. However, when we went to the orchard office and inquired as to whether they needed any additional pickers, – we were told that they didn't need any additional help. Obviously, we were very disappointed. It was now a few minutes after 9:00 o'clock. We did the only thing we could to do – started walking west on Route 40 toward home! I remember the long climb up Sideling Hill Mountain, down the other side and finally we reached the road leading to the farmhouse where we had left our bikes that morning. After walking another mile or so, we got on our bikes and rode the five miles to our home! Yes, we were tired when we finally arrived!

Home from Boot Camp

A couple years after that walk I remember riding a Blue Ridge or Greyhound bus over the same route – this time I was wearing a navy uniform on my way home for my first leave after boot camp. I got off the bus at Little Orlean's Road, it was un-named then, it must have seemed to other passengers on the bus that I got off in the middle of no where. I threw my sea bag over my shoulder, it had all my clothing in it and every thing else I owned, and started walking the five miles to my home. It was a hot day in mid August, and at that time the road was not paved, instead, it was dirt and very dusty! I walked past Ralph Smith's home, a family whose children I had known from school days. Still roughly three miles from home! I was grateful for the shade provided by the tree lined road. I continued walking until I crossed Crooked Run Bridge. Another half mile or so of walking and I crossed the Sideling Hill Creek Bridge. A short distance from that spot I walked past my grandparents' home. I didn't stop; I wanted to get home. One more mile to go – I was warm and sweating, but I don't remember being tired. Finally, I'm home! My mother was in the kitchen – and I remember my little sister, Jerri, coming down the steps from our upstairs –her long blond hair on one side of her face sticking to her cheek. It was apparently warm in the house, too. I don't remember seeing my little brother at that time – he was only about two and a half years old. I do remember him a short time later paging through my Blue Jacket's Manual a bit aggressively and in the process tore a couple pages. I wasn't bothered by it but my mother was – she immediately found the scotch tape and made a mend, which incidentally, is still in place today!

Revisiting Old Swimming and Fishing Holes

Sign identifying the location of Northcraft, Pennsylvania

On this October day in 2006, I continued my drive on Route 40 until I came to Orleans Road. I turned north just as I had done more than sixty years before. However, today it was blacktopped, considerably wider and there were many more houses along either side than had been there when I walked it with a sea bag over my shoulder. I soon came to the home of a family where several of my schoolmates had lived – the house was still standing, but the barn was no longer by the side of the road. I soon crossed Crooked Run Bridge, Sideling Hill Creek Bridge and past what used to be my grandfather Northcraft's home. Today there is an official road sign that reads, Northcraft. For many years there was a post office and general store on the premise. Neither is there anymore – only the sign as a reminder of what was.

As I traveled on past my grandfather's place I thought I'd like to photograph a couple of my old fishing and swimming locations on Sideling Hill Creek. I stopped at what was generally known as the Rock Hole; I remembered fishing and swimming there. The water was quite deep just below a huge rock that seemed to jut out of the hillside right down into the water. A few feet on either side of the rock the water was shallow.

The Rock Hole

A half mile or so farther down the road, an overgrown path along Trough Run led to another favorite fishing and swimming hole. Everyone called this the Katie Hole. I walked down to it and took a few pictures and reminisced about the spot. I had fished there many times with my great uncle, Ross. His father was a Civil War veteran. I would ask him questions about his father's service in the war; he was also my great grandfather. My great grandfather was in The PHB –The Third Maryland Regiment – The PHB stood for The Potomac Home Brigade. My great grandfather lived in Pennsylvania, very close to the border between Pennsylvania and Maryland. My uncle told me that the main reason his father enlisted was "to protect the home front." He would also tell me tales he had heard when his father would be visited by some of his Civil War comrades. Uncle Ross was good at mimicry – and using the tone of voice and peculiar inflections and hand gestures of the person whom he heard tell the tale, he would recite parts of the stories he remembered. One that I remember is this: Ross would state the person's name – and then the tale would begin, "We knew the rebels would be coming soon, so we placed two cannons side by side. Some one had found a long log chain. We loaded the cannons with powder and stuffed one end of the log chain down one cannon barrel and the other end in the other barrel. Soon the rebels came and when they were close enough, we fired; we really mowed'em down!" Good story! But I suspect, untrue. Think of the precision that would have been needed to have both cannons fire simultaneously!!! It is possible it might have been tried, but with success?? I doubt it.

The Katie Hole

I enjoyed swimming at the Katie Hole. It was at the mouth of Trough Run and silt would wash down the run and be deposited on the bottom of the pool. But the water was rather deep in places, but shallow water was never very far from the deepest parts. I would swim from the Katie Hole down to the next deep pool that was several hundred yards downstream. I felt like a long distance swimmer!!! Some of the water between the two deep pools was rather shallow –with an almost vertical cliff on one side. Years later I would go back to the Katie Hole on a camping experience. I'll write about that in another section.

The Old School House

I went back to my car and decided to visit my old elementary school, Barnes's Gap. My mother and all her siblings plus many of her cousins had attended this one room school. In fact, within a stones throw of this school was the location of the one my grandfather and most of my great aunts and uncles had attended, but the building itself had long since disappeared. My old school wasn't very far away – just up the hill a few hundred yards from where my car was parked. The school house was still standing but it had been converted into a dwelling many years ago. It was painted or covered with some kind of shingles, blue in color, I looked at the conversion but in my mind's eye I could see still the white school house that I attended over seventy years ago. The large oak tree that used to be on the edge of the schoolyard along the road that ran by the school was no longer there, nor were the two outdoor toilets that scores of youngsters had visited for many years! I'll have more to say about Barnes's Gap school later.

Barnes's Gap School converted to a dwelling

The Foot Bridge across the Creek

While I'm here, I thought, I would drive down this familiar road—I noticed it now had a name, Hixon Road – but, still unpaved. I wanted to photograph the footbridge that crossed Sideling Hill Creek. The school did not have a well. We carried a bucket of water up this road from the farmhouse that was on the other side of the creek. That was our drinking water at school! The only way we could cross the creek was to walk over the footbridge. The footbridge was supported by four cables across the stream – two bottom cables provided the support for the wooden treads and the two top cables also provided support and a hand hold, if needed. There were vertical rods, as I remember, connecting the top and bottom cables. It was safe enough, I suppose; children who lived on the opposite side of the creek had to use it every day to get to school. I remember crossing it with friends more adventurous than I was. They would make it move side wise as well as up and down by their excessive movements while crossing. Each time we needed a bucket of water for our water cooler at school two boys would ask for and receive permission to go for a bucket of water. The weight of the full bucket of water was shared by two boys running a four foot strip of wood under the bail and carrying their load back to the school house.

I noticed immediately that the steps leading up to the platform where one stepped onto the bridge were missing. The only remnants of the footbridge were a couple of iron supports to which cables had been attached. Apparently the footbridge had been disassembled and removed years ago. Evidently if there are children of elementary school age living on the other side of the creek today, they are transported by vehicle to their assigned school. The traffic on the Hixson road is not sufficient to support a bridge across the creek at this point – instead vehicles using the road must still ford the creek, just as they did when the road was established.

From the location at the site of the old footbridge, I could look across the road to the cliff where my mother and I picked a certain kind of wild flower that grew in abundance among the rocks. She would take the plants home, transplant them to her flower garden and they would continue to bloom and grow.

Driving up Negro Mountain Road

I turned my car around at this point and drove back Hixon road, by the old school house and down the hill to where it intersected the main road. I took this road for about a half mile and made a right turn on what is now called Negro Mountain Road. I don't know when it was named Negro Mountain Road. I suppose it was given that name because it eventually ascends a relatively small mountain that has long been called Negro Mountain, I don't know why the mountain was so named. As a boy I walked this road every day on my way to and from school, at that time it did not have an official name. Maybe we called it the mountain road. We called this particular section of the road, "The Big Hill" My boyhood home was the first house on the left side of the road when traveling north. The "Big Hill" was a great hill on which to sled ride – the big problem, though, was what do you do when you got to the bottom? (It was also a nightmare for cars attempting to ascend it when covered with snow or ice – especially if the car did not have snow chains on the rear wheels!) When I rode my sled down that hill I had one of two options when I got to the bottom. Since the "Big Hill" intersected the main road that ran east and west, the rider of the sled could attempt to guide his sled in either of those directions! Depending on sled speed the rider probably didn't make a successful turn either way! Several years ago the "Big Hill" intersection was improved considerably by having separate exits and entrances where it intersected the main road for east and west travelers. Certainly this would have been a great improvement to any of us who would ride our sleds down this hill.

Nearly all roads in that part of the county at that time were unpaved. After a heavy snow, especially if it were accompanied or followed by high winds, the roads were drifted shut. No snowplows came rumbling through to open them, either. They were opened by men with shovels! It sometimes took several days before back roads were again passable for automobiles. In the spring time when the weather would warm up it seemed that the bottom would

My home

drop out of the road beds. Deep ruts made by automobiles traveling on the muddy roads would be axle deep. These ruts would be smoothed over a little later in the spring and summer by a local farmer who had been hired by the highway department or township to "drag" the roads – using a piece of machinery that was designed to be pulled behind a team of horses. The blades could be angled in such a position as to fill in the ruts and make the road smooth again. The roads were very dusty in the summer. A heavy cloud of dust was raised every time a vehicle drove on these roads. Any porch or lawn furniture left uncovered would always have a coating of dust on it.

The Shanholtz Place

I continued north on Negro Mountain Road past my old home. About a tenth of a mile from our house was the home of the Shanholtz family. The house that I remember is no longer standing; it burned several years ago. Nor is the barn still there –it was torn down long ago. I was particularly fascinated by the barn's appearance during the 1960's when I would visit my parents. I'd always look out our kitchen window in the direction of the barn – the large sliding barn door was painted red. The rest of the barn had never been painted!

The Shanholtz Barn – only the barn door was painted

I had a great deal of respect for Mr. and Mrs. Shanholtz, our neighbors. I would never have addressed either of them by their first name, even after I reached adulthood; it was still Mr. and Mrs. Shanholtz!

Mr. Shanholtz sold some of his farm produce to customers he had in Cumberland, Maryland. Each week he would make the trip. Apparently he brought home with him newspapers –

perhaps some of his customers gave him their Sunday papers. I remember how pleased I always was when Mrs. Shanholtz would pass on to me the "funny papers". I looked forward to that treat! The Shanholtz family was a very good neighbor to us. I have only positive memories of them. My sisters and I still recall their visits to our home – before visiting they would often send one of the boys to ask our parents if the time of their visit would be all right. A memory of Mrs. Shanholtz that I will always have is seeing her working in her garden. I'm certain that some of those vegetables she tended so well were taken by Mr. Shanholtz to his customers in Cumberland, Maryland.

I remember vividly the last time I saw Mr. Shanholtz. I was visiting my parents one Sunday less than a year after my son was born. I put him on my shoulders and walked the short distance to the Shanholtz home. Mr. Shanholtz had been quite ill and, I believe, at the time nearly blind. After Mrs. Shanholtz invited us in, I said to Mr. Shanholtz, "Mr. Shanholtz, this is my son, Jeff." He smiled in the direction of Jeff and then said to me, "Billy, when they are small they step on your toes; when they are older they step on your heart."

Three of the Shanholtz sons, Julian, Lee, and James served in the military during World War II – James also served in Korea.

Julian *Lee* *James*

A new, modern house is now on the property – A grandson of Mr. and Mrs. Shanholtz, son of Julian, lives there. One of the biggest surprises I had on my drive up the mountain road was to see llamas grazing in a field across from where the original home was. I remember only cattle there.

Llamas grazing where I remember only cattle

Buck Valley Ranch

I continued up the mountain road. The next property I saw is now known as the Buck Valley Ranch. It's currently a guest ranch – if one types, Buck Valley Ranch into a search engine on the computer, an excellent description is given of the accommodation and activities that can be experienced here. However, I remember three previous owners. The first owners that I remember were Mr. and Mrs. Frank Lee. Shortly after we moved "up on the hill" Mr. Lee died as a result of a farm accident. The next owners were my aunt and uncle, Zoe (Doll) and Bill Fischer. They moved there in 1941, I believe. Homer, their son, was a senior in high school and finished his last year at Warfordsburg High School. Many years after I had moved from the area Bill passed away at a relatively young age.

I visited with my aunt and uncle many times and ate many meals there, as well.

One hot summer day I was helping Bill thrash. The thrashing machine was in the barn and for some reason Bill wanted the small door opened that was just below the peak on the end of the barn. He said to me, "Bill, how about climbing up there and opening that door?" I said, "Sure," " I can do that." I had every intention of opening that door. I started the climb – using the braces in the corner to get as close to the door as possible. About four feet below the door was a brace or plank, about six inches across that I had to shuffle my way over to get to the door. I was very conscious of the long drop down to the barn floor; there was nothing to hold on to as I started side stepping toward the door. Suddenly, I lost my nerve – I nearly froze in place! I just couldn't force myself to move one step farther out on that plank to get to the door! Slowly, I reversed my side steps and made it back to the corner braces where I could climb back down to the barn floor. I believe I said something like, "Sorry Bill, I just can't do it."

The Buck Valley Ranch
Former home of Bill and Zoe Fischer

I noticed later that it had been opened, I guess Bill did it. Bill was an interesting person. I'll have more to say about him later. Homer, his wife and family, plus his mother lived there quite a number of years after Bill's death. Eventually Homer sold the property and moved to a new location.

Bill and Pearle Karns' Home

After moving up the road past the Buck Valley Ranch I looked up the lane where Bill Karns and his wife, Pearle used to live. Bill was a friend of mine; I liked him and Pearle very much. One of the last times that I visited with them, Bill pointed out the spot across from his house where he had shot a large black bear. He also related some interesting facts about the "moonshine" he used to make. "It had a nice amber color," he said, "and it tested nearly 100 percent." The sign of good distillation, I guess.

One summer I worked with Bill on the orchard picking peaches – I rode with him to the orchard each morning and back home each evening – a distance of about thirty five miles round trip. I recall how generous he was; he wouldn't let me pay him anything for my riding along. There was another incident that reflected on his helpfulness – it was a very cold winter day when he was walking by our house. He stopped and with out being asked, shelled a very large bucket of corn that we would use to feed our chickens and inquired if there was anything else he could do. I'll always think very positive thoughts when I drive by the lane leading up to the house where Bill and Pearle used to live.

My Great, Grandparents' Home

Farther up the lane and beyond the Karns' home a couple hundred yards, was the home of my great grandfather and great grandmother, Joseph and Elizabeth Smith. When I was a boy the old house was still standing. I remember the huge chimney that was on the end of the house. Apparently, at one time there had been a large fireplace –perhaps a cooking fireplace in that room. My great grandmother died in the early thirties, shortly after we had moved from Pittsburgh. My older sister told me that Grandma Lizzie had died and that they would put her in a wood box! My frame of reference for a wood box was what I had seen on my grandfather's porch – crude wooden box in which firewood was kept. That evening when my parents went to my great grandmother's house to pay their respects, I fully expected to see Grandma Lizzie in a wood box similar to the one on my grandfather's porch!

Their son, Ross, had lived with his mother after his father died. Following great grandmother's death no one lived in the house. Everything remained the same as it was at the time of her death. Several years later when I would be walking in that vicinity I would look through the kitchen window and see the table, chairs, stove, everything as it had been when great grandmother was living. I especially remember seeing a 1932 calendar on the wall.

Joseph Smith was my great grandfather and a Civil War veteran. At the age of 21 he joined the army on February 8, 1862 at Warfordsburg, Fulton County, Pennsylvania for a period of three years. His physical description is given as 21 years of age, five feet, eight inches in height, fair complexion, brown eyes and sandy hair. His occupation is listed as a farmer He served in the 3rd Regiment of the Potomac Home Brigade as a private. He missed one muster in April of 1863 because of illness.

Apparently, he reenlisted as a veteran volunteer on February 29, 1864 at Ellicott Mills, Maryland. According to military records, he received the first installment of a $400 enlistment and bounty bonus. This young soldier was to have a 30 day furlough in his state before the extension of the original term. His military record also indicates that he owed the government $2.45 for equipage lost and destroyed in the Battle at Monocacy Bridge. His name appears on the Company's Muster Out Roll in Baltimore, Maryland, dated May 29, 1865. Evidently more ordinance was lost and destroyed; he now owed $18.00, plus the $2.45 he owed for lost equipage at the Battle of Monocacy Bridge! (Perhaps that money would come out of his bonus and bounty) He died in 1916. He continued to work his small far for as long as he lived.

Pvt. Joseph Smith PHB Maryland 3rd Regiment

Lewis and Belle Wigfield's Place

I continued my drive up the road. My great Aunt Belle and Uncle Lewis Wigfield lived in an unpainted house about a tenth of a mile beyond the lane leading up to Bill Karns' house. Let me describe the property and the couple as I remember from many years ago. The house had never been painted and as long as I can remember was in a state of some disrepair. The side porch had a distinct slant to it. The grass was pretty high and the shrubbery around the house had not been trimmed in many years. There was a path from the edge of the porch to a crude building over a spring that served as a washhouse. The spring was the source of their drinking water.

Aunt Belle was a couple years younger than her sister, my grandmother, and Uncle Lew was several years older than Aunt Belle. I can remember his riding past our house on his horse, which he called Dan. We lived about a mile from his house. My Aunt Belle would visit my home when my mother had a quilt in a frame and my great aunts and my grandmother plus other friends of mother would spend an evening or afternoon "quilting". Mother said that she could look at the quilts and identify who had made each stitch.

Painting of Lew and Belle Wigfield's House

I often rode my bicycle to Uncle Lew and Aunt Belle's house. Aunt Belle was always there – usually in the kitchen; her kitchen always smelled like maple syrup – she must have used a lot of it. My sister, Aggie, also walked to Aunt Bell and Uncle Lew's home often; Aunt Belle was always very congenial and very pleased to have visitors. However, Uncle Lew very often would not be there – especially if he had seen anyone approaching whom he thought was going to stop and visit for a while. He would frequently hide until the visitor left; then, he'd come out of hiding! One day, however, he apparently hadn't seen me ride my bicycle up to the house. I walked up to the porch where he was sitting and spoke to him – he was a bit surprised to see me, but he was very congenial. Several years before my mother had taken me along to a funeral she attended, the funeral of a Civil War Veteran. The Civil War Veteran was my Uncle Lew's older brother. After a couple minutes of small talk about the weather, the dusty road, and how hot today was, I asked him a question about his brother having been in the Civil War. He said to me, "Yes, he did serve in the war, but he didn't want to go." He went on to tell me how his brother had hidden in the chimney of their house. It seems that their house had a large fire place, which was not uncommon for farm houses of that era, and the chimney rising above it was very large. "His brother", he said "hid in the chimney that day until the men who came looking for him left the property. He was pretty dirty, I guess, when he crawled out."

The couple had two children – a son and a daughter. The daughter died relatively young and left four children. Three of her sons lived with the father; the daughter, however, at a very early age, went to live with an aunt near Pittsburgh, Pennsylvania. I remember when she used to visit Aunt Belle and Uncle Lew. I'm certain that her visits were very much welcomed and appreciated by both. Perhaps her grandsons also visited – I just never saw them there. I do remember their son driving by our house on his way to visit his parents many times. A vivid memory that I have of visiting in their home was one Christmas Eve. I went with my parents – a small kerosene lamp was on their kitchen table, no signs of any Christmas decorations, Uncle Lew was in bed – he always went to bed very early. My mother had taken some cookies, probably a cake to give them – we wished them a Merry Christmas and went home.

My Aunt Belle died several years before Uncle Lew did – after that the old man lived by himself. My mother and others, including my two younger sisters, often took him food that was ready to eat. After his wife passed away he was much less apt to hide when visitors came to visit. Unfortunately, he apparently had never learned to cook. Sometime during the late 1940's two of my cousins stopped to see him one morning; they found him dead, lying face down on the floor.

As I drove by their property I saw no evidence that the house is still standing. Trees, weeds and thick underbrush covered what used to be the yard. The fence that enclosed the yard. was no longer there, either. Apparently, too, the large catalpa tree that stood directly in front of the house died and decayed many years ago. I recall Uncle Lew riding his horse, Dan, to our house and giving my mother a catalpa seedling that probably came from around the base of the large one in his yard. We planted it in front of our house – it matured and provided beautiful blooms in the spring and produced those rather hideously long bean like pods in the fall. It did not have a particularly long life, however.

Scott and Emma Smith's Place

The next house still standing on my journey out the mountain road was where my great Uncle Scott and Aunt Emma lived. Until a few years ago, perhaps a quarter mile before getting to Scott Smith's place, there was a house known as the Northcraft lodge. There were never any permanent residents living there – instead, it was built, owned, and visited occasionally by people living in or near Pittsburgh, Pennsylvania. Unfortunately, it burned to the ground –only the fireplace chimney now stands. I never knew the cause of the fire. It was in the field, just beyond the Northcraft Lodge property and not far from Uncle Scott's house where Henry Lee was shot and killed. That event is discussed in another section of the book.

Uncle Scott was my grandmother's brother. He and his wife were both very interesting persons. Uncle Scott was fascinated with Indians – he had pictures in his house of many different Indian chiefs from different Indian tribes of the south and west. I remember one afternoon when I stopped to talk to him he gave me quite a dissertation on how one could tell the difference between an Indian's bone and a white man's bone. He also told me that he was part Indian! I mentioned this "bloodline" to my Uncle Ross, Uncle Scott's brother, once and his very skeptical response to me was– "Why is it that he is the only one in the family with this Indian connection?" Another time when he was in a more jocular mood, he said to me, "Yes, we're part Indian, our grandmother was Granny Fleetfoot, known as fastest runner on the mountain!"

Uncle Scott told me how he used to tease my grandmother when she was using the spinning wheel. Apparently in their family they had a large "walking wheel" that was used for spinning wool. He explained how it was used – my grandmother, as a small girl, would use a short stick to strike a spoke of the wheel to make it rotate; then when she would walk backward to allow the wool to twist into yarn on the spindle, he'd tug at her hair to distract her! Apparently boys teased their sisters in the 1880's, too!

Scott Smith's house as it appears today –
During the 1930's and 40's it was unpainted

My sister, Aggie, and I visited the couple one day, had dinner with them and when we left they gave us a pair of bantam chickens. We named the bantams, Scott and Emmy! The Smith property was located just before the road begins its ascent of Negro Mountain and where Trough Run emerges from between Negro Mountain and Ray's Hill or Big Mountain, as it was referred to in that location. My Uncle Mike Northcraft took me coon hunting up the trough (between the two mountains) one night – it was cold, kind of spooky, made more so by the barking of those big black and tan hound dogs we had taken along. I was glad when we made our way out of the trough and headed home!

It was in Uncle Scott's rye field, not too far from his house, that the murder of Henry Lee took place. I recall my dad, when driving past the location, would always mention what had happened there. One time he took me into the field to show me the exact spot where the shooting occurred. I write about this tragic event in more detail under another heading in the book.

Buck Valley Hunting Camp

During the 1930's and early 1940's deer hunters would gather at Scott Smith's house to organize their hunt. I remember hearing automobiles traveling past our house, early in the morning, on the first day of deer season on their way to his home. The above picture was taken in 1939. From left to right, back row: Mike Northcraft, Lee Shanholtz, Ted Northcraft. Middle row: C. Beatty, S. Smith, Bill Karns, Leo Northcraft, W. Barnes, Homer Fischer, Ralph Smith, Earle Clingerman. Bottom row: G. Clevenger, Bill Fischer, D. Lehman, Scott Smith

As the picture above indicates, the nimrods had a successful hunt! Hunting, for the great majority of residents in that general area, was a very popular sport. I suspect it still is!

After taking some pictures of a "renovated" Uncle Scott and Aunt Emma's house, I continued my drive up Negro Mountain Road and drove to two other locations I wanted to photograph: the Veteran's Memorial, erected to honor persons who had served in the military, and Center School, a one room school house currently used for township business.

Memorial to Servicemen at Buck Valley Park

Memorial to Veterans

The Memorial is located in a beautiful setting – on the grounds of a Methodist Church established in 1882 but has not been used as an active church since 1950. An old cemetery is located behind the church. Several names of veterans whose names are on the Memorial are buried in the cemetery. Across the road is Buck Valley Community Park, a site that has been used for community functions and reunions for many, many years. I recall going there many times for reunions or picnics of one kind or other. At one time there was a ball diamond in an adjacent field.

As I stood in front of the Memorial and read the names of men who had served in the military during the Civil War, World War I, World War II, Korean War, and additional names of veterans whose names were not associated with a specific conflict, I could not help noticing how many last names were the same in each war!

There are 36 veterans listed from the Civil War. This is a large number considering the rather small population of this community during that era. Most of the soldiers were from small farms: they had very limited financial assets; therefore, few were able to "buy" a substitute. Some enlisted or re-enlisted because of the bonus money they could receive. Some of these veterans had only recently immigrated to this country. Their names appear in the Federal census of that era as having been born in a country other than the United States. This listing may not include all veterans who lived in this general area during the 1860's; some names could have been missed.

I counted the names of 37 World War I veterans on the Memoral. I knew many of them. There was the name of our mail carrier for many years, Marshall Siegel. He had a rural route and drove by our house six days a week I don't believe he ever missed a day! I noted Harry Fischer's name, brother to my uncle, Bill Fischer. I had visited in Bill and Harry's mother's home many times. I recall seeing a World War I helmet on the wall behind the stove in the kitchen of Mrs. Fischer. There was Ralph McKee's name, husband of one of my favorite teachers, Ada McKee. I saw the name William Oakman, father of Marvin and Lamont. Marvin was one of my best friends in high school. Marvin and Lamont's names are on the Memorial, both served in the military. Interestingly, William's brother, Oscar, was a World War II veteran who was killed in that conflict. Another name from the World War I list that had a special significance to me was that of Charles Stahle, Sr. I had gone to high school with three of his sons, Gene, James, and Charles, Jr. (known as Tom) James and Tom did not graduate with their class in high school, instead at the time of graduation they were serving in the military. James served in the Pacific theater and Tom served in North Africa and was badly wounded in the invasion of Italy. They received their high school diplomas in absentia. There were many more World War I veterans whose names I recognized. Persons that I had known as a boy while growing up in the community.

It was an emotional experience for me to look at the names of the World War II era servicemen. Each recognized name presented in my mind's eye a person who will always be forever young! I still see him as a member of a high school or community baseball team, a high school basketball squad, or a track team. I remember where many of them sat on the school bus that we rode to high school. I remember where each one boarded the bus in the morning and where each one got off the bus in the afternoon.

I looked at the name, Ernest Hendershot. I saw a blond haired high school student that I sometimes sat next to as we rode the school bus to and from Warfordsburg High School. In January of 1945 he was killed in action in Belgium. George Miles was another name I recognized. His mother, Mrs. Ada Miles, had been born in Buck Valley but she and her family had been living in California. In the late thirties or early forties the family moved back to the area. They moved to a home not too distant from my home. Mrs. Miles rode the school bus to the Warfordsburg School, where she taught for many years as an elementary teacher – the school served both elementary and secondary students. Her son, George, was an early enlistee in World War II; he was one of the first young persons in the area to lose his life in the war.

I mentioned above that the Stahle name had a special significance to me. I knew the Stahle family quite well. On the school bus Tom (Charles) and Jim (James) sat in a middle seat – I sat on a side seat opposite them. They were two happy fellows. Each participated on athletic teams in high school. During their senior year in high school they, along with others in their class, entered the military. Tom was severely wounded in the invasion of Italy. He survived several operations and after his recuperation was assigned duty in Pennsylvania at POW camps. He performed this duty until he was discharged. Tom was reluctant to talk about his military experiences. He did relate to me once what the situation was the day he was "hurt," as he put it. He was to lead a squad to recapture some of "our men" who had been captured by the Germans. A mortar shell landed in his vicinity and he received multiple wounds in the back, legs and abdomen. Fortunately, Tom was a strong farm boy who was able to survive the initial surgery of a field hospital and subsequent surgeries elsewhere.

Several of the names on the Memorial had been students at the little one room Barnes's Gap school, during the time I attended there. Included among those names were brothers from the Smith family, Wayne, who served in Europe during WWII and was the recipient of three bronze stars, Grant, also served in WW II, and Donald served during the Korean conflict. George served during a later period. Albert, Marvin, and Bruce Mann served during WW II, as did the three Shanholtz brothers, Lee, Julian and James. I also recognized the name of Guy Weicht, another young man who will be forever young in my memory. I saw him one time after he was a student during the 1935-36 school term.

Below is a listing of all the names that currently appear on the Memorial. I am certain that since the last name was added to the bronze marker, many more young men, and women have entered the military from that area.

Names of Veterans on the Memorial

Civil War

Issac Barney
Charles Hendershot
Henry Beatty
Robert Beatty
George Hoopengardner
Charles Bowden
Morgan Burton
Henry Lee
Robert Carson
Isaiah Lehman
George Schetrompf
William McKibben
Peter Mellott
Joseph Smith
John Miller
John Parlett
John Taylor
Thomas Parlett
George Fischer
Andrew Gienger
Samuel Hendershot
Jacob Gienger
Jacob Hamman
Joseph Hoopengardner
Daniel Hebner
Fred Hebner
William Lee
John Potter
Levi Potter
Jacob Schetrompf
Bazil Powell
David Richards
Daniel Smith
John Schetrompf
Peter Schetrompf
Ephraim Whitfield

World War I

Calvin Beatty
Charles Hoopengardner
Chester Bishop
Chester Cavender
Glenn Lehman
Elmer Cavender
Guy Crawford
Kenneth McKee
Harry Creek
John Deneen
Harry Fischer
Oscar Lashley
Orben Hebner
Ray Hendershot
Arthur Lynch
Walter Hendershot
Clive Hixon
Ralph McKee

Francis McKibbin
Raymond Schriever
James McKibbin
William Oakman
Edward Olschiski
Orville Schetrompf
Stanley Schetrompf
Earl Potter
James Ray
James Richards
Charles Ritz
William Ritz
Marshall Siegel
Charles Stahle, Sr.
Clyde Stahle
Charles Schetrompf
John Wigfield
Claude Schriever
Walter Wigfield

World War II

Fred Barnhart
Ernest Hendershot
Herbert Barnhart
Clyde Beatty
Lester Deneen
Ralph Beatty
Siebert Beatty
Lloyd Hetterman
George Beckman
Floyd Bohrer
McKinley Leasure
Gerald Burlington
Elmer Carson
Bruce Mann
Albert Cavender
Gene Cavender
Harold McKee
Robert Clark
Dale Clevenger
Quay Mellott
Stanley Crawford
Ludwig Creek
Charles Deneen
Herman Deneen
Harold Hendershot
Lewis Hendershot
Sheldon Deneen
William Hendershot
Marshall Divel
Homer Fischer
William Hoopengardner
Clyde Fletcher
Leslie Flickenger
Albert Mann
Carl Frisel
David Hann
Marvin Mann
Clarence Hendershot
Claude Hendershot
Herbert McKee
Clyle Hendershot
Donald Hendershot
George Miles
Earl Hendershot

Donald Murray
Marvin Oakman
Oscar Oakman
Hayes Ward
James Orr
Chester Ray
Glenn Ward
Ernest Ray
Dale Ritz
Paul Ward
Rolla Romm
Blair Shetrompf, Jr.
Guy Weicht
Clark Scriever
Homer Scriever
Reed Scriever
James Shanholtz
Julian Shanholtz
Lee Shanholtz
Foutz Shank
Claude Ward
Leroy Shank
Woodrow Shank
Herbert Ward
Earl Sigel
Grant Smith
Grant Ward
Ray Smith
Wayne Smith
Raymond Ward
William Smith
Charles Stahle, Jr.
William Zirkle
Cloyd Stahle
James Stahle
Meade Stahle
Albert Ward

Korean War

Lee Bohrer
Robert Ward
John Elbin
Carl Fletcher
Leon Beatty
Albert Hendershot
Glenn Hendershot
Gerald Hixon
Marvin Northcraft
Willard Northcraft
Lamont Oakman
Benjamin Ritz
Walter Romm

Military Service

William Fischer
Paul Hendershot
Gerald Hendershot
Sylvan Hendershot
Allen Hixon
Jerry Beatty
David Hixon
Ronald Hixon
Lee Lashley
Harper Layton
Melvin Mann
Roger Mellott
Dean Northcraft

Kenneth Scriever
Donald Smith
Andrew Spade
Homer Stahle
Dane Ward
Billy Ward
Robert Ward
Claude Sigel
Ambrose Ray
Elmer Ray
Melvin Romm
James Shank
Vaughn Shank
George Smith
Richie Ward

Methodist Church

Buck Valley Methodist Church

The church was established in 1882 but has not been used for regular services since 1950. There is an old cemetery behind the church; many of the veterans on the Memorial are buried there.

Buck Valley Park

The Community Park and the Game of Baseball

This community park, located across the road from the Memorial, has served for many yeas as a location for reunions, picnics and entertainment of various types. At one time there was a ball diamond in an adjacent field. Later the main ball field for the Buck Valley was located near Ritz Brothers' store.

Baseball was certainly the game of choice for many of the residents of this community. I suspect, in part, because one of their own had made it to the Major League. Anyone of my age, and this was certainly true of older residents who had ever swung a baseball bat, knew or had heard of Clyde Barnhart. Barnhart had played baseball for nine years with the Pittsburgh Pirates. During that period the Pirates had played in two World Series. They won the series in 1925 playing against the Washington Senators. In 1927 they lost the first four games against the New York Yankees. The Yankees at the time were considered unbeatable – on their roster they had such players as Babe Ruth, Lou Gehrig, Bob Meusel, and others. Clyde Barnhart was considered to be a very good hitter. Of the ten runs the Pirates got in that series, Barnhart drove in four of them. He played the infield as well as the outfield. His son, Vic, played for the Pirates in 1940. Clyde Barnhart went to the Shippensburg Normal School – now Shippensburg University.

Center Elementary School

Center elementary school

I remember three occasions when I was inside the Center School house. The first time was when our Barnes's Gap ball team played the team from Center school. What a comical sight our team must have been! Our ages would have ranged from about eight to twelve or thirteen. We had no uniforms, only two or three persons had gloves, our bats were an assortment of homemade and purchased, and we played with a rubber ball instead of a baseball! Our transportation to and from Center School was via the high school bus that picked up high school students at both Center and Barnes's Gap Schools. We played our game during the two recesses and the lunch periods. I don't remember who won, though. I do remember that we got back on the bus in the afternoon when the high school bus stopped at Center School and rode the four miles or so back to Barnes's Gap School. The experience gave us something to talk about for the next several days.

The second time I was in the building was when all the eighth grade students from the four schools of this district assembled to take the eighth grade examination – an entrance examination that one had to pass in order to be accepted for entrance into high school. At the time all the schools in the district were on an 8-4 plan – meaning eight years of elementary, plus four years of high school. I am certain that nearly everyone passed the exam. The following September would be a new experience for all of us as we entered high school. For the last eight years we had the same teacher for all subjects for an entire year. Now, for the first time we would have a different teacher for each subject and move to a different room at the end of each period. We would all be transported by bus to Warfordsburg High School.

The third time I was in the building was after I had been discharged from the service. Because I had enlisted prior to my eighteenth birthday I had never been registered for the draft. However, the summer after my discharge I got a draft notice informing me of the time and place to register. I complied, of course, and was pleasantly surprised to find that one of my former elementary teachers, Mrs. Ada McKee, was the draft board representative who registered me.

Chapter 2

The Murder of John Henry Lee

The Move from Pittsburgh

My family moved from Pittsburgh to Union Township, Pennsylvania in 1933. My father had worked for the Pittsburgh Railway Company. Like so many other men during that era he was laid off from what had been excellent employment. It was a good life for all of us in Pittsburgh. Our family had many modern conveniences, a nice apartment, a new gas stove, a large Philco radio, a washing machine, new furniture; there were stores close by, and best of all, money to spend! But, the decision to move back to Union Township meant leaving most of those conveniences behind. Initially, we moved in with my maternal grandparents. They lived on a large farm; two of my mother's brothers, Mike and Ted, were still living at home as well as an unmarried great uncle, George. Within a year of my family's move a tragic incident occurred to a neighbor living about a mile from my grandparents' home that would impact where we would be living in the near future.

A Shooting in a Rye Field

The family's name was Lee. John Henry Lee was married to Jessie Mellott. Jessie had been a classmate of my mother. They had known each other from an early age. A short time before Mr. Lee's death I remember my mother and I visiting with Jessie at her house; that evening Mr. Lee drove us back to my grandparents' home, a distance of about a mile. Mr. and Mrs. Lee were respected members of the community.

During that era there were people in rural areas that saw an opportunity to profit from prohibition laws, which were in effect from 1920 to 1933. The ridge and valley section of Pennsylvania, with its steep hillsides, spring fed runs, and relative isolation invited a few of the unemployed and small farmers to earn a little extra money by making "moonshine". Those who engaged in this activity were not in any way members of a criminal element. They were simply enterprising persons who needed money and making a few gallons of whiskey was a way of earning a few needed dollars! There were always ready buyers for their product. It was widely rumored by many, and considered a fact by some that Mr. Lee was involved on a small scale in making illicit whiskey. In fact, there was some evidence that he was. A couple years after Mr. Lee's death my father found parts of a still close to a spring, and a partially rotted whiskey cask buried beneath a pile of wooden fence posts on the property. Individuals who were involved in the illicit production of whiskey were always suspicious of any stranger who suddenly came into a community. Perhaps Mr. Lee was no different.

On July 16, 1933, a "drifter" was seen in the area. He had been spotted at a local ball game as well as having been seen walking along one of the country roads. Earlier that evening an unknown man had stopped at the small house where Scott Smith and his wife lived. Their home was approximately two miles from the home of Henry Lee. According to a report in a Chambersburg, Pennsylvania newspaper, Mrs. Smith gave the man something to eat – she also reported that he carried a gun. During this era it was not all that uncommon for drifters or tramps, as they were sometimes called, to be seen on country roads all over the country – thousands of able bodied men were unemployed. Reportedly, he asked for and was granted permission to sleep in Scott Smith's rye field that night. Jessie, Henry's wife, was a niece of Mrs. Smith. Mrs.

Smith was a sister to Jessie's father. The rye had been cut and shocked. Some of the details of the evening that I remembered my father and others discussing were corroborated by Julian Shanholtz. Julian is a brother to Leonard (maybe spelled Lenard) Shanholtz, now deceased, who was with Henry the night he was shot and killed. The Shanholtz family lived in the next house – about a tenth of a mile – from the home of Henry Lee. According to Julian's account, Henry asked Leonard to take him to the location where the stranger was. Leonard did and when they reached the field where the unknown man was, Henry went into the field to talk to him – Leonard remained in his car and had not shut off the motor when an acquaintance, by the name of Roy Siegel, came along in a truck and stopped to talk to Leonard. Shortly thereafter, the two of them went into the field to check on Henry and found him lying on the ground; he had been shot. Leonard did not hear the shot. Nor did either Leonard or Roy see the stranger. He had left the scene. Lee's body was loaded into the vehicle that Siegel was driving and taken to Lee's home. After the capture of the stranger, a couple days later, he told authorities that Lee was shot at a distance of not more than 20 feet; he saw him fall, he said, but did not go to him because he saw a second man and was fearful that he would shoot. According to a report in the *Public Opinion* newspaper of Chambersburg, Pennsylvania, the shooter stated that Mr. Lee had a gun and that he (the shooter) had shot Mr. Lee in self-defense.

After the shooting the "stranger" left the scene and, according to a statement, made after his capture, "circled the mountain and came south". Authorities were notified as soon as possible after Lee was shot and killed. The search for the shooter began. On July 19 the fugitive was captured in West Virginia. He had traveled south in Pennsylvania and crossed into Maryland. Only a narrow strip of Maryland at this point separates Pennsylvania from the Potomac River. He waded across the river. The Potomac River is the boundary between West Virginia and Maryland. He was spotted by West

Virginia authorities who claimed the fugitive had fired at them – they returned fire and wounded him in the arm and foot.

According to the *Public Opinion* Newspaper in Chambersburg, Pennsylvania, he refused to identify himself. His identity was determined when his fingerprint report was received by West Virginia Authorities. He was identified as Walter M. Alley of Brown Branch, Missouri, a 43 year old farmer by occupation. The same newspaper report indicated that he had a pump action shotgun – which according to Walter Alley had been given to him for work that he had done for a farmer in Maryland.

He said he fired at the person in self-defense because the individual confronting him had a gun. On July 19, 1933 shortly after he had been captured, he was taken to Berkeley Springs, West Virginia for immediate medical treatment, from there he was taken to the Martinsburg City Hospital in Martinsburg, West Virginia. He remained there until July 26 at which time he was removed to the Franklin County Jail by Sheriff Roy Sipes.

The Murder Trial of Walter Alley

The trial date was set for October 30, 1933. The prosecution had a list of 15 witnesses; there was none for the defense. It was a short trial – the prosecution presented their witnesses on Oct. 30. The Court convened at 9:00 o'clock in the morning and adjourned at 5:00 o'clock in the afternoon.

It convened the next morning at 9:00 o'clock. Since there were no defense witnesses and the defendant refused to testify or answer questions on his own behalf, the case came to a close. At 12:30 o'clock instructions were given to the jury and at 2:30 they rendered the verdict: Guilty of Murder in the First Degree – Penalty, Life Imprisonment. The judge sentenced Walter Alley to life imprisonment in solitary confinement at the Pennsylvania Western Penitentiary.

There is no question as to whether Walter Alley shot and killed Henry Lee. He did! However, it was widely believed by those who attended the trial, and those who review the record of it, that had Mr. Alley testified at his trial, his sentence may have been less severe. He had apparently threatened no one during his short stay in the area – nor was there any evidence that he was a danger to anybody in the community or anywhere else. He was sleeping in a rye field – where, reportedly, he had asked permission and had been granted permission to do so by the owner.

Just as there is no question that Walter Alley shot and killed Henry Lee, there is no question that it was Henry Lee who visited Walter Alley who was spending the night alone in the rye field! It was he who aroused the itinerant, maybe from his sleep, – and apparently flashed a light on him, (it was dark) and, according to Alley, pointed a gun at him.

Many questions, without answers, could be posed regarding this tragic incident. For example, what was Mr. Lee's motive for arousing this itinerant who was sleeping in a rye field? Was he going to order him to leave? Was he going to question his identity? Did he know that the person sleeping in the rye field had a shotgun? Had he heard rumors that aroused his suspicion with regard to the itinerant? Conversely, what was the frame of mind of Mr. Alley? Did he truly feel threatened by this man who had disturbed his rest, possibly awakened him from sleep? Did he shoot in self-defense? Was he reflecting on his previous arrest back in his home state? (he had a previous arrest) Did he consider that arrests (s) unfair? Was he embittered by events of his recent past, his unemployment? Were words exchanged between the two? Who said what?

Walter Alley chose not to answer any questions at his trial; there were no witnesses to testify on his behalf. Had he been willing to take the stand, maybe some of the above questions would have been asked and answered. He did not take the stand; significant questions were not asked. The consequences of the event that night were tragic; a family was left without a husband and father, and the guilty person was sentenced to life imprisonment. Mrs. Lee and her family left the area shortly after the murder of her husband. She and her family found a new home in the state of Ohio

My mother continued to correspond with Jesse, Henry wife, for many years after she had moved away. I believe, too, that she returned to her former home and visited with my mother a couple of times after leaving Pennsylvania. Mrs. Lee, eventually remarried and evidently lived a happy and useful life in her new Ohio home.

Walter M. Alley's Statement

Reproduced below is the statement of Walter M. Alley of Brown Branch, Missouri. It was taken at the City Hospital in Martinsburg, West Virginia at 8:05 pm, July 19, 1933 in the presence of witnesses and authorities of the West Virginia State Police. It is presently a part of the court record housed in the Court House in McConnellsburg, Pennsylvania.

Q. Have you been promised any reward or immunity to make the following statement or have you been threatened in any way?

A. No

Q. What is your name?

A. Walter Alley

Q. Where do you live?

A. In the state of Missouri.

Q. In what city in Missouri?

A. My father lives in a place called Brown Branch.

Q. When was the last time you were in Brown Branch?

A. Over three years ago.

Q. Are you working anywhere at the present time?
A. No

Q. When did you leave Missouri?
A. In 1931

Q. Where did you go after you left Missouri?
A. I came over to Illinois.

Q. Why did you leave Missouri?
A. I had heard about Illinois being a great state for corn and wheat so I came over.

Q. When did you leave Brown Branch?
A. When I was sentenced to the Jefferson City, Missouri State Prison.

Q. When were you sentenced, Walter?
A. In November, 1929.

Q. What were you sentenced for and for how long?
A. Two years for felonious assault.

Q. When did you get out of prison, Walter?
A. January 26, 1931.

Q. Were you ever arrested after that time?
A. Once for riding a freight train.

Q. Do you recall where?
A. In Parkersburg, West Virginia.

Q. Do you know when?
A. When I came east.

Q. What did you serve that time?
A. Ten days in the County jail.

Walter Alley's mark appears on each page with the name of a witness

Page 2

Q. What was your first stop after leaving prison?

A. I stopped at Springfield, Illinois looking for work in the corn belt.

Q. Where did you go after leaving the corn belt?

A. I came east to Maryland.

Q. What town were you in while in Maryland?

A. I was close to a little town named Dickenson.

Q. What did you do there?

A. I worked on a farm shucking corn. I worked for men named Moxley and McKimey.

Q. Do you know their first names?

A. No

Q. How long did you work there?

A. Altogether I worked around there for about two months.

Q. What did you do next?

A. I went to Washington, D.C. to hunt work.

Q. What month was this?

A. About February 1933.

Q. What did you do from February to July 1933?

A. I worked for a farmer about six weeks near Dickensen.

Q. Then what did you do?

A. I went back to Washington.

Q. How long did you stay that time?

A. About two weeks

Q. After that what did you do?

A. I left Washington and headed toward Pennsylvania.

Q. When you came to Pennsylvania what were you carrying?

A. I had a shotgun.

(Walter Alley's mark appears)

Page 3

Q. Was it in plain view?

A. It was not concealed.

Q. Do you know where you were in Pennsylvania?

A. Not exactly. It was a valley.

Q. Do you know where that valley was?

A. It was not close to the National Pike.

Q. What town did you go through to get to that place?

A. I don't recall.

Q. Do you recall Sunday, July 16, 1933?

A. I don't recall the date, but remember last Sunday.

Q. What did you do on that day?

A. Along in the morning I picked some blackberries along the way. Then I came up across the valley in Pennsylvania and came around where a ball game was being played which I watched awhile.

Q. After seeing the game where did you go?

A. I stopped at several farms and asked for something to eat.

Q. Did they give you anything to eat?

A. Yes, some chicken sandwiches and some jelly.

Q. When you got the meal did you offer to pay for it?

A. At one place I did.

Q. After that where did you go?

A. I came on down the road and at the edge of the valley.

Q. Is this the place where you slept and how far approximately was it from the ball field?

A. This was a mile, more or less from the ball field and in a rye field. I laid down on the rye and laid my gun by me.

(Walter Alley's mark appears witnessed by one of the persons present)

Page 4

Sometime after dark a couple of men came along in a car and they stopped. One man jumped out and came towards me. When I looked up I saw a gun in his hand. I then kneeled and fired one shot at him. I saw him fall.

Q. How close were you to him when you shot?

A. Not over 20 feet.

Q. Did you go up to the man after he fell?

A. No, I saw the other man and was afraid he would shoot.

Q. Where did you go then?

A. I circled the mountain and then came south.

Q. At any time while fleeing did you see any men following you?

A. Yes, I saw three men in a car.

Q. Did they have uniforms on?

A. I could not say.

Q. Where did you go when you started south?

A. I came down the valley and struck an old road that went down to the railroad track and then to the river. I waded the river.

Q. When you waded the river what state did you come into?

A. West Virginia

Q. How do you know you were in West Virginia?

A. I had been in West Virginia several times and crossed the Potomac River.

Q. Do you also know that the Potomac River is a dividing line between Maryland and West Virginia?

A. I knew the river was a dividing line.

(Walter Alley's mark appears)

Q. Did you see a car after you crossed the river?
A. After I crossed the river I met the car coming and set my gun down on the ground.

After the car passed by I picked my gun up and came on and crossed the mountain and went on until I got to the second mountain. There I saw a farmer feeding hogs and told him they were after me and told him to tell them to come and get me. I started on up the mountain when two or possible three men appeared.

Q. Did these men call you to halt?
A. I do not recall.

Q. Then what happened?
A. When they started shooting I dropped down and then they shot me in the arm. They say I shot, but I don't remember.

Q. How many loads were in your gun when you started up the mountain?
A. One in the barrel and two or three in the magazine.

Q. What happened to you after the shooting?
A. They brought me to Berkeley Springs, West Virginia where I received medical treatment and from there they brought me to this hospital in an ambulance.

Q. Do you read and write the English language?
A. Yes

Q. Have you read the above statement and is it true and correct to the best of your knowledge?
A. Yes.

Q. Is there anything that happened that you have not mentioned in the above statement to the best of your knowledge?
A. No

(Walter Alley's mark appears)

After having read the above statement and being told that anything I may say in the above statement can and will be used against me in my trial in court I willingly sign it.

The statement is signed with his mark X and his type written name below.

It is also signed by six witnesses with the usual legal statements made on such documents: State of West Virginia, County of Berkeley.

Subscribed and sworn to before the undersigned authority by the aforesaid, Walter M. Alley, this 19th of July, 1931 as witness my hand and notarial seal

Signed by the Notary Public.

It is quite apparent that Mr. Alley was not represented by council during this interview. I was puzzled, too, why he made his "mark" when in the statement he said he could "read and write" the English language!

Chapter 3

Living in the New House

Moving to Our New Home

Shortly after Mrs. Lee had moved away my maternal grandfather purchased the small farm that had been owned by the Lee family. My parents moved to it in March of 1934. A short time before they moved the well-constructed barn, built by Mr. Lee, mysteriously burned. No clues or information as to how the fire was set or what motivated anyone to set it was ever publicly advanced. Could it have been deliberately set by a disgruntled, disappointed, would be buyer? The secret of the fire's origin – if caused by an individual – was buried with the individual many years ago.

View from our front porch

I remember quite well our move to the new home. The house was located on a hill. Actually, it was on a ridge and the road that ran by our house made it descent for about a half mile down to a major road that ran east and west at a considerably lower elevation than our house. The view from the house was wonderful. We could stand on the front porch and see Ray's Hill on our right and look toward the west through Barnes's Gap into Bedford County. From the same

View of the gap in Sideling Hill Mountain and West Virginia

place on our porch we could look through the gap in Sideling Hill Mountain into West Virginia. It was through this gap that the Sideling Hill Creek flowed into the Potomac River. The B&O Railroad and Western Maryland Railroad also ran through here. In the winter time when the atmosphere was just right we could easily hear the train whistles blow as they would pass through that area. My dad used those train sounds as a predictor of stormy or snowing weather to come. If we looked toward the south or slightly southeast we would be looking at land in Maryland and Townhill Mountain.

Combined chicken house and pig pen

The only outbuilding on the farm when we moved was a combined chicken house and pig pen. The barn had burned a short time before our move. Several years later I helped my dad tear it down

A Description of the New Home

Our house was not an extremely large house. There were three rooms down stairs and four rooms upstairs. Our kitchen was large with a deep well hand pump in one end. The kitchen, a later addition, was build right over the well. Along one wall there was a wood-burning kitchen stove. The exterior of the house was unpainted.

Apparently, Henry Lee had built an addition to the house when he and his family moved there. Another room, part of the original house, was used as our living room in which there was a sofa, two large overstuffed chairs, a wood burning heating stove, and a couch that my uncle had made for my mother. It was a plain couch that looked more like a small bed; oak sides, oak legs and very sturdy. For the first year or so that we used it, my mother made a mattress for it that was stuffed with clean straw. The couch was covered with a heavy, hand made quilt.

Linoleum was used as the floor covering – I remember when the wind blew very hard we could see the linoleum rise and fall on the floor. The front porch was open underneath and faced the south and southwest; it took the brunt of winds – especially in the winter and spring.

The third room downstairs was empty, initially, a bare floor, a door without a doorknob, unheated, and for the first year or so that we lived there, used very little. There were four rooms upstairs – three of those rooms were above the original structure, one was over the kitchen; the new addition. Since there was no central heating, obviously the upstairs was quite cold in the winter time. Thank goodness for the heavy woolen, home made quilts that we all used on our beds!

But despite the lack of creature comforts, all of us – a family of five, were very happy to have a place of our own. My oldest sister, Alta, was nearly nine years old, I would soon be six, and my younger sister, Agnes, was three. This would be my home for the next eleven years. In retrospect, they were very good years, despite the lack of money in the household and lack of conveniences that nearly everyone today takes for granted. Our lighting came from kerosene lamps – not very bright, but sufficient to read by and for my mother to do whatever domestic chores that needed to be done at night. At one time I remember she bought a gasoline mantle light because she thought the bright light from it would make it easier for us to do our school work – but, she was afraid to use it for fear that it might explode or cause a fire! Obviously, we had no electricity, no telephone, no indoor plumbing, no automobile for the first couple of years that we lived there and very little outside entertainment, and initially, no radio. The closest town was about twenty miles away, and we didn't go there very often, either, but there were plenty of positives, too. We learned to provide our own entertainment, there were games to be played – card games, checkers, Chinese checkers, songs to be sung; food was always plentiful, we were all very healthy – and for a boy, there were woods to explore, streams in which to swim and fish, and a neighbor who had a couple boys who would be boyhood playmates. And somehow or other, I always had books to read. An extra bonus that I did not realize at the time was the close proximity of my maternal grandparents, uncles and aunts, as well as great uncles and aunts. Plus acquaintances from earlier generations that reflected values that helped shape my life. I got to know all of these people quite well. Fortunately, many of them lived to a ripe old age and I knew them not only from the perspective of a child, but also, from the perspective of my young adulthood.

Life Improves

As time went by, some of the harsh realities of the first few years were modified – my dad got a car, yes an old one – a 1926 Oldsmobile sedan, we bought a "farm" battery operated radio, and furniture was moved into the bare unused room. A new floor was laid down in the living room and the west winds no longer lifted the linoleum in that room. For a few years my dad was employed as a highway maintenance worker –until there was a change in the political structure of the state –then he, and several others, were laid off and employees of the "winning" political party were hired to replace those who had worked during the previous political administration.

If one were to describe the larger community where we lived, using today's social language, undoubtedly it would be described as, "depressed". It was an area of small farms and it would appear that very few families could be described as being affluent. Perhaps that is why, as a family, we never felt "poor"!

We always had plenty of food, we had a very large garden, plenty of vegetables to eat during the summer and my mother canned the surplus for use in the winter. We got peaches from nearby orchards and mother canned many, many quarts of them. We had our own meat – mostly poultry and pork. Our clothes were not tattered rags –they may have been "hand me downs," or sometimes home made, but I guess we weren't that conscious of the latest fashions.

The school that we attended was a one room school of eight grades – certainly anyone who would have looked carefully at the twenty or so students occupying the classroom could not have discerned much difference in the way the students dressed. Most of the boys wore overalls and, perhaps wore a pair of "high top shoes" –if lucky, had a pair of high tops with a little sheath on the side of the shoe top that contained a small pocket knife. Many of the girls wore either home made clothes or, perhaps, those bought from a mail order catalog.

The packed lunches that everyone carried would not have varied much either – peanut butter sandwiches, egg sandwiches, ham sandwiches, if it were in the fall of the year after hog butchering had occurred, fresh meat sandwiches; pies, maybe pumpkin, apple, cherry or whatever the mothers had made for the family that week would have been found in many of the lunch boxes. I remember I often had cold chicken in my lunch on Monday because we had chicken on Sunday! From my grandfather's general store my mother would sometimes get cans of "potted meat" or Vienna sausages from which to make our sandwiches – potted meat cost five cents a can and a can of Vienna sausages cost ten cents! Very few children had sandwiches made from bought bread –most children had sandwiches made from homemade bread! Heavy, thick slices, that, as my mother would have said, "Will stick to your ribs!"

Our First Car

Our first car was a 1926 Oldsmobile sedan. It was bought used from a resident who lived just outside our little community. There weren't too many miles on it – something like 15,000, but perhaps for that era that many miles would certainly have represented the most trouble free miles of a car. Especially, if one considers the state of the roads over which it would have been driven. The distances the car had to travel after dad bought it at any one time would not have been very far – to and from the local stores, not more than four or five miles away, to visit relatives, again less than five miles away, and for my dad to drive to and from work, which would not have been more than five miles away. The longest trip we ever made in it would have been to Hancock, Maryland – about twenty miles.

One feature about the car that I remember very well was an interior light that was attached to the dash. Nothing more than a bulb over which there was a metal sheath studded with blue and red glass. When the light was turned on it cast blue and red light on the ceiling of the car's interior. Across the back of the front seats was a hinged bar that one could grab if seated in the back and use as an aid in getting out. I was resting my arm between the bar and the front seat where the bar was attached one night when we were going down a dirt road about a half mile from home. My dad got too close to a small tree on the right side of the road. The right fender and right corner of the wood and cloth car top hit the side of the tree. In a matter of seconds we had a car without a top, no windshield, and a car that would never run again. Fortunately, nobody was seriously hurt. Apparently because my arm was between the bar and rear of the front seat when we hit the tree, the impact badly sprained my arm. The glass in windshield must not have been safety glass – my mother had several pieces in her coat pocket.

The Next Car

Our next car was a 1933 Oldsmobile. During the time my dad owned this car it probably spent as much time waiting to be repaired as it spent on the road. It must have been very anxiety producing for him to drive this vehicle on even the shortest of drives! And I didn't help matters a bit – I discovered that as we traveled down the "Big Hill" from our place to the main road, always in second gear, I could sense the rhythm of tire rotation. For some demonic reason I would tap my feet on the floorboard of the car in rhythm with the rotating tires. To my dad the knocking sound must be coming from the engine! He was always expecting something about the car to malfunction. He would say, "Listen, listen, what is that sound?" Obviously, he wasn't too pleased when he would learn that it was "Billy" kicking his feet on the floorboard. Following an episode of that type my dad would give a quick assessment of my intelligence!! It was always on the negative side of the Bell shaped curve!

Eventually dad stored the car in our barn and purchased a 1936 Oldsmobile that gave him better service than either of the other two Oldsmobiles. By this time, in the early forties, he was working in Hagerstown and had enough confidence in it to make the approximately 60 mile roundtrip once a week!

For several years the 1933 Oldsmobile remained in our barn. Sometime prior to my sixteenth birthday dad thought he might have it fixed for me to drive when and if I got my license – at 16. On a Saturday he and I decided to tow it out of the barn. He hooked one end of a fifty foot steel cable to the rear bumper of the 1933 Oldsmobile and the other end to his 1936 car. The 1933 Olds had been stored in the barn with the front end toward the end of the barn.

The barn was located on a relatively steep slope and, as I recall, we needed to place a couple thick wooden planks on the ground in front of the barn floor so that there would not be too much of a drop off from the floor to the ground. After all those necessary preliminaries were taken care of – he gave me my instruction. All I had to do was keep the front wheels straight and when we got to the top of the hill and he drove his car through the gate, I was to steer the car through the gate. Backward, of course!

Seemed like a very simple task to me. I got behind the wheel of the 1933 Oldsmobile and my dad started the engine in his car. He had made certain that my car was in neutral and the emergency brake was released. In a few seconds the slack was out of the cable and my car was moving backward out of the barn. We had done a good job in placing the planks just outside the barn floor When the rear wheels left the barn floor, I wasn't even aware of it. Soon we were moving slowly up the slope toward the gate.

Suddenly I heard a snap and my car reversed its direction! I'm heading right back toward the open barn door onto the barn floor! I jammed my left foot on a pedal – The car kept right on moving, closer and closer to the barn door opening. Frantically, I turned the steering wheel to the left and I coasted to a stop with the front end of the car headed slightly up grade on the hill where only a few seconds before I was slowing being pulled backward.

Before I could get out of the car my dad was on the left side of it, waiting for me to get out. Not very happy, was he! "Why didn't you hit the brakes," he said. He didn't wait for me to say, "I guess I must have hit the clutch pedal" "I'm surprised you didn't run it back onto the barn floor and out the other end," he said, as he walked back to his car. He never again mentioned getting the car fixed for me to drive – nor did he ever invite me to drive his! I wonder why!!! Eventually he sold the car – I do not remember when or to whom. I think I have blocked out of my memory the 1933 Oldsmobile!

My youngest sister, Jerri,
sitting on the running board of Dad's 1936 Oldsmobile

Radios and Entertainment

I mentioned above that my family bought a battery operated radio. It was ordered from a Sears Roebuck Catalog – Their brand name was Silvertone. It used a single battery pack that fitted into a space in the rear of the table model that we had. I remember we had a wire antenna that was approximately 15 or more feet above ground. A 2x3 strip of wood about 12 feet long was nailed to one of the post that provided fencing along the side of the garden. One end of the antenna wire was connected to the top of the 2x3 strip and the other end to the outside of the house several feet above the radio.

The antenna wire ran down the side of the house and was connected to the lightning arrester, which was screwed to the side of the house. Another wire ran from the radio antenna post to the lightning arrester. A ground wire was run from the arrester to a metal post driven into the ground along side of the house. I don't know if the radio was connected to the antenna correctly or not, but that's the way my dad and a friend connected it.

As I remember all that was left to do was connect the radio to the battery with a plug and cord and the radio was ready for use. I believe the battery was supposed to last for 700 hours, or perhaps more, depending upon how much was paid for it. Our radio had a short wave band which I enjoyed listening to. It was on this tabletop radio that I listened religiously to "Tom Mix," and ate plenty of Ralston so that I could buy the gadgets that were "pitched" at the beginning and end of each program. I wonder if I still have that TM bar ring that I sent a dime and proof of purchase from a box of Ralston to whatever address listed? Then, there was "Jack Armstrong, the All American Boy." Again, I ate Wheaties, sponsor of the program, so that I could send a box top and a dime for one of the many little gadgets that were available from that sponsor.

I would not have missed an episode of the "Lone Ranger" for anything! This was probably my favorite – I doubt if there is anyone over the age of 65 or 70 who wouldn't recognize the "William Tell Overture" that was used as the music on the Lone Ranger program—and the strong voice of the announcer as he would say, "from out of the past comes the thundering hoof beats of the great horse Silver, the Lone Ranger rides again." And at the end of the program someone would say, "Who was that masked man," and another actor would respond by saying, "Why that was the Lone Ranger" – then, we would hear the Lone Ranger say, as he and Tonto rode away, "Hi Yo Silver, Away!"

Of course, there was "Little Orphan Annie" not really one of my favorites, but I did like Ovaltine, the program sponsor, and I remember ordering some of the merchandise that was available by sending a dime and some proof of purchase of a jar of Ovaltine to the address given by the announcer.

It was also on this inexpensive tabletop Silvertone radio that my older sister listened to the "Lux Radio Theatre of the Air" – I recall my dad grousing about draining the battery when she would be listening.

My younger sister, Aggie, rushed home from school so that she could listen to one of the radio soap operas, such as "Portia Faces Life"! On Saturday nights I would listen to the "Grand Ole Opry," out of Nashville, Tennessee. Or a similar country music program broadcast out of Wheeling, West Virginia. Those radio artists never knew it, but I sat on a chair beside our Silvertone and on my little mail order guitar attempted to play right along with them!

On certain nights the entire family listened to Fibber Magee and Molly, Jack Benny, Amos and Andy, Lum and Abner, and a host of others.

Probably one broadcast that I remember best is the one that occurred on December 7, 1941 – I had been out in the yard playing when I came into the house and the announcer was discussing the attack that had occurred at Pearl Harbor. Later that afternoon when I went to our woodpile to carry in the night's supply of fire wood – the thought occurred to me, "Suppose we lose this war?"

That night a young Lee Shanholtz, one of our neighbor's sons came to our house and talked about the attack. Before too long after that Lee was serving in the United States Army. On Monday morning, December 8, I went to school as usual. I recall that my first class was Latin. Another student in the class, a young girl who sat opposite me in the next row, looked over at me before class had begun and said, "Is it really true that our country is at war?" Apparently her family did not have a radio. From that date on one of the greatest functions of our radio was to listen to the news given by such persons as Gabriel Heatter, Lowell Thomas each evening, and Walter Winchell, on Sunday night.

Our 1930's Silvertone battery radio

The Wind Charger

And speaking of radios, at my grandfather's house, where two of my uncles lived, they had erected a platform behind the house on which they placed a "Wind Charger." It looked liked an airplane propeller from a distance – as the wind turned the blade the shaft was connected to a generator – from which a charge was sent down the wires to a 6 volt storage battery that, as I recall, was set on a bench behind the kitchen stove. They had two batteries – one would operate the radio until it became weak and then it was replaced by a charged one. The two batteries were rotated as needed. This system worked fine – as long as the wind blew!

I remember my grandfather and a great uncle, three years older than he, sitting in their living room, lighted only by a small kerosene lamp and in the winter heated by a Heatrola stove listening to "Amos and Andy" and "Lum and Abner," two very popular programs during the mid thirties and into the forties. Since my grandfather owned and operated a small general store, I suspect he could identify quite well with the dialog he heard on Lum and Abner in their little store in Arkansas!

Our neighbor, Mr. Frank Shanholtz, had a radio before we did. I recall going with my family to the Shanholtz house to listen to the first Joe Lewis and Max Schmeling boxing match. Mr. Shanholtz had certain conveniences that most families of the area did not have – he had a 32 volt electrical system. There was a small structure close to the house that sheltered a set of batteries that provided limited electrical power for household usage. Apparently electric light bulbs were made to operate on a 32 volt system and, of course, his radio.

The Importance of Music

Music played an important role in our early years "on the hill." For a few years we had no radio – we created our own entertainment. We sang! One of my early memories of singing was one evening when we were singing a song – probably a hymn; I dragged out the last note of a measure for such a long time that my dad was prompted to say, "Billy, I could walk to the barn and back before you're ready to start the next line." But, lack of ability did not deter me from wanting to sing.

My sister Alta and I learned a song taught to us by Vera Foster, a teacher, who had some musical ability, and who may have been in charge of the Children's Day service at the small country church we were attending at the time. I don't remember the name of the song, but the first line began with "When Samuel was a tiny lad –There were several verses and we learned them all. I guess you could say that was our signature song! Alta sang the lead and I sang the harmony in a little boy's high soprano voice – tenor, I think my dad called it. We sang it many times, at home when company came, or even if we didn't have company! My aunt, who was a teacher in a small elementary school in an adjoining county, even asked us to sing it there, which we did!

That little boy soprano voice was wonderful – high notes, low notes and everything in between. Absolutely no strain – the alto part, the lead, the high notes were no problem. Gosh, how all of that changed at about 13 years of age!!! When the voice started to change I was never certain if a sentence would end on the same vocal pitch on which it started or not – my voice seemed to have all the quality and timbre of a young crow practicing his call! Finally, the voice stabilized, but that wonderful range that used to be there, never returned. Nor did the confidence to sing in front of a group – always afraid the voice would play "tricks" on me!

But sing we did for several years before my onset of puberty – yes, our music repertoire did increase, we learned a few more songs to supplement –"When Samuel Was A Tiny Lad!" Did my mother sing? Well, mom had a vital flaw in the genetic component of her musical make up – a problem in carrying a tune! Jokingly, I'd say, "Mom, why don't you just clap your hands, instead of singing." But, I still remember mom singing while sitting on the side porch rocking my baby brother! He didn't care whether she was flat or sharp – he enjoyed it, I'm certain. She sang him to sleep. I suspect she probably sang the same song, in the same way to her other four children when they were babies. She probably sang all of us to sleep! What's that old proverb – "He who wants to sing can always find a song!" And you don't have to be able to sing well, to enjoy singing, either!

As a small boy I remember going to picnics or reunions and a group of local persons would provide entertainment by way of music. There may have been four or five person playing a guitar, a fiddle, a banjo and perhaps a mandolin or second guitar. The individuals playing and singing did so with gusto! What the musicians lacked in musical skill, talent and knowledge was more than made up for in spirit! The music was loud and fast – the songs may have been learned from their parents, or learned from 78 rpm phonograph records. Not necessarily the latest from Tin Pan Alley!

Very early I wanted to play a musical instrument. My first choice at about the age of five was a violin. I believe my mother was dissuaded from buying the violin because her Uncle Ross said the violin sounds made by a kid like me would be very difficult for everyone to listen to! Ross played a violin and I guess my mom considered him quite knowledgeable on such issues. She got me a ukulele instead. Well, that was fine – I played more with it, than actually playing it. Fortunately for all, it wasn't very loud nor was it very sturdy – it collapsed before I learned many chords on it.

When I was about eight years old I wanted a guitar very much. My parents ordered a three quarter size guitar for me from a Montgomery Ward catalog. The cost was $4.25! I was ecstatic with this little guitar. I studied the instruction book that came with it like I'd never studied anything before. I learned to tune it – following the instructions given in the book; then I began placing my fingers on the strings to form chords. I guess the skin on my fingers was too soft to press the strings against the frets with enough pressure to form sound – my chords didn't sound like music – more like a weak thud!

But, I persevered. The chords began to sound a little better – perhaps because I now had calluses on the tips of my fingers! I practiced all the chords that were in the instruction book religiously. And yes, I accompanied myself when I sang songs – mostly in a back room downstairs where in winter time there was no heat – and the walls muffled the sound! I did fine as long as the songs had no more than three or four chords in them! I played this little guitar for about four or five years and really wanted another one –a full size guitar.

Mail order catalogs of the day usually had a pretty good selection of guitars and other stringed instruments. I did not know it at the time, perhaps it would not have mattered to me if I had, but the guitars sold by the mail order catalogs were made primarily by the Kay and Harmony Company. Most of them were low-end guitars – that arrived to the user with a pick, and an instruction book. A case was sold extra. Nearly all of them should have had a "professional set up" before the owner attempted to learn even the first chord – I suspect if that had been the case, more recipients of these guitars would have learned to play. By set up I'm referring to making the instrument somewhat easier to play. Often the strings were too high off the frets for easy fingering – especially if the learner wanted to play closed chords further up the fingerboard.

Today if one looks at the fingerboard of these guitars that have survived the years, it will be noted that nearly all the wear is on the first three to five frets – From the fifth fret toward the body of the guitar the strings are so high above the fingerboard as to make it nearly impossible to play.

My Guitars

Again, it was from a Montgomery Ward catalog that I ordered my next guitar. I waited rather impatiently the four or five days until it arrived. This one was definitely a step up from the first one – The cost, just a little under $10.00 – Actually, the one ordered was not in stock so the firm substituted a better one, it cost $12.25!!! A spruce, sunburst finished top, curly maple back and sides, an ebony fret board, celluloid binding around the top and bottom edges, really, a rather handsome guitar. But, if one were to judge its playability by the standards of most low end guitars today its rating would be pretty low. The action was high, and higher as one went up the fingerboard toward the twelfth fret. I soon discovered this as I attempted to play closed chords at different positions on the guitar fingerboard.

My first guitars

My seventh grade teacher, Mrs. Ada McKee, had taught me the letter names of the lines and spaces on a piece of music and I had learned how to determine in what key the music was written. – I knew the letter names of the six strings of the guitar. With that elementary musical knowledge I was ready to teach myself to play the guitar directly from a sheet of music! Well, it turned out to be a very slow, and laborious process.

First, I had to decipher the notes from the sheet music and jot them down on a piece of paper. Next, I located those notes on the guitar fingerboard – it took so long for me to get to the end of the measure that the melody was unrecognizable! I think I gave up trying to sight read and stuck to songs I already knew – much easier and a lot less frustrating to me. However, I still envy those people who can look at a musical score and immediately transfer that knowledge and skill to a keyboard or fingerboard!!!!

Fortunately for everyone I had a long hiatus from the guitar starting after my mid teens until after retirement! Yes, I still have those first two guitars – joined in recent years by a stable of about sixty others! Do the additional guitars mean that I can play any better today? Probably not. Oh, yes, I still practice but practice doesn't always equate to improvement; perhaps I practice the same mistakes I made as a young teenager! But, I still love music and continue to play.

A New Sister and At Last, a Brother

When I was eleven years old our family increased in size – I now had another sister! Jerri arrived one night in May and was immediately everyone's favorite little girl! She was certainly mine – very pretty with her blond hair and blue eyes! I was in the seventh grade and having a baby sister was wonderful.

I recall that I sent her picture to some firm that I had heard about on the radio that would take the face on a picture and embed it into a finger ring.(Cost, 50 cents) I waited and waited and at last the ring arrived. I wore it for awhile and then put it away. Many years later I gave it to Jerri, that baby sister, who was now grown. Oh, for years I wanted a brother, but after a few weeks with the new sister, the desire for a brother was waning. Besides, I was eleven years old and a brother at this time wouldn't be able to play ball, go fishing, hike in the woods, or do any of those things that I always fantasized doing with a brother!

Eventually, the brother, Leon, would arrive – but by then I was fifteen years old! Actually, he and I didn't live under the same roof for very long. I was sixteen years old when I graduated from high school and didn't spend too much time at home after that.

Jerri and Leon, even though they had the same biological parents that their older siblings had and lived in the same location, experienced life in a quite different environment. Our parents were generally more affluent during this time period of their life. Television was available as entertainment, there were more frequent visits to larger stores – and most importantly, more money to spend! Their childhood was lived in a post World War II era. Plus, as parents grow older they mellow somewhat. It often seems that privileges that have to be fought for and won by older siblings are handed out free to the younger siblings. Then, too, for better or worse, there is the influence that older siblings have on younger brothers and sisters.

In retrospect, I wish I would have spent more time with my two younger siblings. I do have some memories – one in particular that reflects how little I understood toddlers! I was in the navy and had just done some Christmas shopping with one of my buddies. I told him I had a little brother who was not yet three years old. He asked me what I had bought him for Christmas. When I told him I had bought a pair of boxing gloves he couldn't wait until he told everybody we knew that "this dummy bought his three year old brother a pair of boxing gloves." Of course, he was right! Not a very appropriate gift for a little boy.

Perhaps I did a little better as he got older – I remember taking him a small puppy one time. A few months later I visited my parents and a sad little boy told me his puppy had been killed that day – run over by a car.

Yes, I remember taking him and Jerri to a county fair. We had a great time. I recall how he laughed when the three of us got on one of those rides that twisted and turned, spun around and made the stomach feel as though it was turning upside down.

Poor Jerri, didn't fare so well. We started home after the ride and hadn't gone very far from the fair ground until her little stomach was, in fact, turning upside down! She was pretty nauseated and – almost green in color! I stopped the car, she got out and "upchucked" whatever junk food we'd had at the Fair! They still remember that day. And, so do I!

Christmas at our House

Christmas at our house was probably the most memorable holiday. There was never very much money – but everyone always had gifts under the tree. We always had a tree. We'd go into the woods near the house and cut either a white pine, which my mother preferred, or one of what my dad called, a "Jack pine" – coarse, sturdy, stiff needles and not particularly nicely shaped. But we decorated either kind with the glass balls, tinsel, and icicles that were kept in the "Christmas Box." This box, made out of some kind of very tough fiber, remained in the attic from about a week after Christmas until it was brought down again about a week before. Actually, our tree looked great to us kids.

A practice that was quite common where we lived – usually a few nights before Christmas, was Bellsnicklers or Kris Kringlers coming to the door. Several person would come together, dressed in silly, disguised clothing – and the home owner would attempt to guess their identity.

I remember one such visits. We were in the process of decorating the tree and I had found an old, child's chamber pot somewhere in the house. I guess I thought I was being funny but I set it directly under the tree in full view. Mom hadn't seen me do it, or she would have removed it very quickly. Our visitor came into the room and my parents identified them. Only after they left did mom discover the chamber pot that I had set under the tree! A bit embarrassed, was she!

We'd go to Hancock, Maryland to do Christmas shopping, and for a quarter I could buy gifts for the entire family – my mother, dad and my two sisters. At that time Jerri and Leon had not joined the family! I would buy dad a comb for a nickel, a wash cloth for mom that would cost a nickel or maybe a dime, and a dime would buy two handkerchiefs for my two sisters! Of course, long before December 25 I would have perused the Christmas catalogs distributed by Sears Roebuck and Montgomery Ward – we had both, and identified several items that I really wanted. I loved toys – and my parents always seemed to find enough money to buy each of us something that we "really" wanted.

I still recall my sister Aggie and I going down the steps to the living room on Christmas morning where there was a wood burning stove – my dad had "banked" the fire before our going to bed, and the door to the living room had been closed. This room on Christmas morning – probably at six o'clock when Aggie and I arrived, was quite comfortable, at least compared to the rest of the house! On this particular Christmas morning my parents had bought me a wind up, mechanical train. Before going to bed mom had put the track together, wound the engine motor, set the engine and cars on the track and all I had to do was move that little switch on the top of the train engine and around the track my train traveled! There were many Christmas mornings similar to that.

My mechanical train

Mom's Christmas Dinners

My mother loved to cook and bake; she prepared wonderful meals. None was ever better than her Christmas dinners. Apparently she began several weeks before the holiday with her baking. She would have different types of cakes including the usual types of "fruit cakes," another that I liked she called an "apple sauce" cake. It was very moist, with lots of raisins in it. Still another that was a favorite with all was called a popcorn cake. It was a mixture of various kinds of nuts and pop corn held together with some kind of caramel syrup. Then, there were the pies: minced, pumpkin, cherry, banana cream in some kind of graham cracker type crust and I'm certain there were others. Nor were cookies slighted – raisin filled, ginger, sugar, peanut butter, chocolate chip are some that come to mind! And other types of desserts – I couldn't begin to recall all of them – I remember the banana desert that appeared to be layered in some kind of graham cracker mix, jello was the base for some of her desserts, fruit salad, and of course whipped cream, I mean the real kind, was always available for those who wanted even more calories!

The usual turkey with filling always had a place on the table. But, there were also baked ham, plus a large plate of fried oysters – a separate dish of oyster "stuffing" was present, too, for those who liked it! I didn't. Mashed potatoes, candied sweet potatoes, corn, peas, cranberry sauce, red beets, baked beans – table space was the only limiting factor for mom's dinners.

It was after such a dinner that the story I'm about to relate occurred. I was no longer a boy though, I was an adult, married, as were my siblings. It was pretty much a tradition with our family that everyone went home and had Christmas dinner with mom and dad. It was a house full – five married children and spouses, with, at that time, one grand child.

Dinner was over and I was standing by the table. Our kitchen at home was a large one and always served as the dining room. The living room was where the Christmas Tree stood and was the scene where gifts were unwrapped. Paper was strewn on the floor and many conversations would be going on at the same time. For a short period of time the room appeared as though a tornado had swept through! But, today the gifts exchange had taken place earlier, we had eaten dinner and now my mother was in the process of clearing the table.

Dad's Watch

While standing beside the table my dad walked up beside me. Without ceremony he pulled his watch out of his watch pocket, handed it to me and said, "Here, I want you to have this, I carried it for thirty seven and a half years and it served me well. Maybe someday you'll want to give it" – his voice trailed at this point and he didn't finish the sentence. I suspect he almost said – you'll want to give it to your son. On that Christmas Day I did not have a son. Our child was not born until the following March. He may have wondered about the word "son" – after all, the expected grandchild could be a grand daughter!

At the moment of dad's presentation, I remember my mother saying to him, "Well, Roy, you might have put it in a box and wrapped it!" He made no response – he had done what he wanted to do.

Since that gift on Christmas Day in 1954 the watch has served an important service in my life. Not as a time piece, my wrist watches have provided that function, but rather it has helped me to chronicle important events in my life as well as his.

Apparently he came into possession of the watch in July of 1916. In his late teens he had taken a job in nearby

Cumberland, Maryland with the railroad. Evidently he needed a railroad watch. It was a handsome time piece, a 19 jeweled Waltham Railroad watch. In order to set the time on it, one had to unscrew the bezel that held the crystal and then lift a tiny lever located under the watch crystal, before turning the stem to move the watch hands. Dad would jokingly say, "When you want to set this watch you shouldn't plan on doing anything else the rest of the day!" It was a reference to the difficulty that one sometimes had in screwing the crystal back onto the watch.

I thanked my dad for his gift and took it home with me. I soon bought a glass enclosure, with a lid, and decided I would use it as a display item. However, it occurred to me that perhaps I would carry it on my person on occasions that I deemed to be very important. That first occasion was the day/night my son was born. I was teaching in a school about ten miles from where we were living. At lunch time I was called to the telephone; it was a call from my wife. She thought it was time for her to go to the hospital. I wasted no time leaving the school and driving to the location where we were living. We were living in a mobile home – probably less than five miles from the hospital. A quick call was made to my wife's obstetrician, I put my dad's watch in my pocket (I thought this was a very important event!) and we were off to the hospital.

About mid afternoon my wife's doctor came into the waiting room and told me that I might as well go home – it would be a long wait for me. He suggested that I give him a call that evening. I did, but he was still somewhat indefinite as to what time the baby would be born. I pulled my dad's watch out of my pocket; seven o'clock, it said. I got into my car and in a few minutes I was sitting in the waiting room at the hospital near the maternity ward. I started reading the magazines in the waiting room. I would interrupt myself every thirty minutes or so to check at the nurses' station to see if there was any "news"! I guess I read just about everything in the waiting room – excepting one magazine that had a lengthy article in it about the country of Brazil. It was now about one thirty in the morning.

I started reading the article about Brazil and soon decided that maybe sometime I could use much of that information if I ever had to develop a unit of study on that country. So, I started copying information on a clean sheet of paper I found in the waiting room. Suddenly, the doctor appeared in the door way! "You have a fine looking son," he said! "When can I see him," was my response. "Soon," was his answer and he disappeared. I looked at my watch – two o'clock! In a few minutes a nurse came into the waiting room carrying the little guy – red faced, sleeping very comfortably, so it appeared to me. I visited my wife in her room and then went home. It was now about four o'clock in the morning. I went to bed, got up in a couple of hours and met my students. I was tired and sleepy, but happy!

Dad's watch was placed back in its glass enclosure and continued to be a display item for the next few years.

I guess one might say that the watch served as my "security blanket" – we had moved to another location and on this particular night I was to be interviewed for an administrative position in a new school district. I put the watch in my pocket and drove to the location of the interview. I seated myself in the waiting room with a couple other candidates and waited! After a while a secretary came to the room and said something like, "They are ready to see you." I looked at the watch – seven thirty o'clock. The interview went fine – I got the job.

A few more years would pass before I needed my "security blanket" again. It was the day I was to take my written examination as part of a doctoral program in which I was enrolled. I went to the specified location, a secretary directed me to the office where I was to take the exam. She handed me a list of twelve questions – the directions at the top of the sheet said, answer any eleven! I looked at my watch – eight o'clock. I started writing – time went by quickly. The next time I looked at the watch it said, twelve o'clock! "Time for lunch," I said, and walked to a little restaurant about 15 minutes away.

By one o'clock I was back in the office continuing to answer some of the remaining questions. As I finished answering the last of the eleven questions and made a cursory review of what I had written – some fifty pages, I noticed how quiet everything was. I looked at the watch! It's now eight o'clock. Wow, I thought, I've been here all day! I placed my papers in the secretary's inbox – left the building, grabbed a sandwich and went back to my room. Again, very happy the exam was over.

I would carry the watch again some months later when I had to take my oral comprehensive examination in front of my committee who would fire questions at me from all angles for nearly an hour. This ordeal also turned out all right for me. I remember when the session ended; outside it was snowing – nearly a blizzard condition. I drove to my home, nearly fifty miles – I didn't mind the snowy, icy road at all. I was very happy. It was eight-thirty that night when I drove into my driveway.

After the better part of a year during which I had completed writing my doctoral dissertation I had to defend it before the committee that had aroused so much anxiety in me in the two previous exams. I looked at the watch. Eleven o'clock, it said. That gave me a little comfort – I reasoned that they probably would not continue the questioning for more than an hour – those professors had to eat, too!

The questioning began – a visitor from another academic department was in the room as a spectator. After each committee member had exhausted his/her prepared questions, I was dismissed and told to wait in the adjoining room until a decision was made. The visitor left with me. He was very comforting – "You've nothing to worry about," he said. I hoped he was correct. I looked at the watch eleven forty five! A minute or so later the committee chairman came out of the room and said, "Congratulation, Dr. Smith." I assumed I had passed.

Several years would pass before I would carry the watch again. This time it would not be a happy occasion. My father had passed away – I carried it to his funeral service. I also carried it to my mother's funeral five years later.

Today it sits on a shelf in its glass enclosure. Each time I look at it I'm reminded of significant events in my dad's life. And, I wonder – Did he check what time it was when he got his notice to appear for a physical prior to induction into the army in 1918? When he came down with the flu a few days before the induction date and his induction was postponed to November 15, did he check the time? Did he check his watch at eleven o'clock on November 11, 1918 and think, "Maybe my induction will be cancelled!" It was. In October of 1923 when he and my mother were married – out of nervousness, if nothing else, I'll bet he pulled the watch from its pocket many times! Did he check the time, as I did, when his children were born – I'm certain he did.

I wonder what his thoughts were as he checked the time on the last day of work when he was furloughed from the Pittsburgh Railways.

The next nine years would be tough ones for him – we were in the midst of the Great Depression. I wonder what he was thinking at the end of each day when he wound his watch! I do recall the desperation in his voice at the end of one day. We had driven a mile to visit someone and when he got out of the car he said, "God, I'd rather be dead than to live another year like the last one!"

But we all survived those depression years – and after the beginning of the 1940's life got much better for my father. Yes, he still carried that watch – it survived a fall down our stair steps and, eventually, one part of the case wore through. He had the watch enclosed with a new case.

When anyone asked my dad what the time was – he didn't answer with something like ten fifteen, or fifteen minutes after ten – Rather it would be more like fifteen minutes and thirty two seconds past ten o'clock!

It will continue to sit on a shelf, protected from dust in its glass enclosure – until I give it to my son. Perhaps someday he'll want to give it to his son. My dad would have liked that!

Chapter 4

Family Life in the Smith Household

I would like to believe that my sisters exaggerate when they remind me of some of my antics as a boy, but, in truth, I remember too many of them to deny any of their accusations. And, I was probably more obnoxious than their memories recall and fortunately, my own memory, because of embarrassment, has blocked the recall of the worst.

Shadow Boxing in Front of the Glass Door

I do remember, though, the day I decided to shadow box in front of our kitchen door. It was a common kitchen door with a large panel of glass in the top half. My "opponent" was my reflection in the glass – but the image had probably morphed into someone who was a danger to me and everyone else in the family. This was a chance to slap him around a bit! My footwork was great – I danced, feinted with both hands at times, slipped punches – the guy I saw in the reflection never touched me!

Nobody was in the kitchen at the time so I had complete freedom to beat this bad guy up! I was doing great until I decided to use a triple jab, very fast, I thought – but, the last of the jabs wasn't pulled in time! I actually hit the bad guy in the reflection smack on the chin! When I did about half of the glass fell out of the frame – some jagged pieces remained. The fantasy was over – I had just knocked the glass out of the door. How do I get out of this one? There's only one thing to do – tell mom what I was doing! It went better than I thought – no threats, no severe scolding or anything like that. I know she told my dad but I don't remember that he appeared too upset. I do recall that a neighbor, Bill Karns, measured the opening and when my dad bought the glass, Bill installed it. I didn't shadow box any more before a glass door or a mirror. I did, however, stuff a burlap sack with balls, rags, and whatever I could find and suspended it from the ceiling on the porch and punched the devil out of that contraption. But, no more boxing in front of glass doors or mirrors.

Mom's Tolerance for My Antics

Mom was mild with regard to this incident, but I remember another time when I think she'd really had it with me. She was making lemon pies and I must have been teasing her or one of my sisters. I'm not surc anymorc "what thc straw was that broke the camel's back," but mom unleashed a volley of lemons at me—I believe she had three in the air at one time – not one hit me as I ran for the door and down the steps and off the porch. Mom had a strong arm, a quick release, but was terribly inaccurate!

Mom was usually pretty tolerant of my indiscretions – but, that didn't mean that I got away with too much. For example, I had a sheep skin coat when I was in the first or second grade that I had to wear to school when the weather began to get cooler in the fall. It was a very warm coat and usually that warmth was appreciated in my walk to and from school a distance of one mile. But there was this day when it was quite cold in the morning, but by dismissal time that afternoon it had warmed up considerably. After dismissal I started toward home with the other kids that walked in the same direction. About a half mile from the school I started the last half mile up a steep hill to my home. By then I was getting very warm – instead of taking off my coat and carrying it over my shoulder, I had another idea. I would get rid of the coat! There was a woods along side the road where

I was walking. I took my sheep skin coat into the woods and threw it down at the foot of a good size tree. I walked home in comfort; by the time I walked through the door at my home I guess I had forgotten about my coat.

The first question my mother asked me wasn't about my school day, but rather an abrupt, "Where's your coat?" I was never good at fibbing – so I answered truthfully, "I threw it away." A puzzled look was on her face. "Where did you throw it?" " Under a tree at the foot of the Big Hill," I said. There was no long wait for her response – "You march right down that hill and get it." I did!

Mom bought some other clothes for me that I never threw away, but I certainly wanted to. Knickers! They had to be the very worst clothing that mothers ever bought for little boys. I hated them with a passion! Second on my list would have been those Lindberg helmet type hats – they came with goggles that snapped in place on the front of the hat – and the goggles could be moved down over the eyes. I guess I didn't mind the hat the first few times I wore it – but as soon as the novelty of the goggle wore off, I detested it! I believe I used to take the straps that went under my chin and pull them up over the top of the hat and wear it that way. I can remember how my head would sweat in the darn thing and the inside of the hat would be damp when I removed it, the outside of the hat must have been covered with some type rubberized material. Then, if I put it back on a few minutes later it would still feel damp.

As I indicated above mom was pretty tolerant of some of my behaviors. There was another time when I invited a friend from school to spend the night at my house. That was fine with my mother. Only a few weeks before she had wall papered the entire kitchen. Ours was a large kitchen and papering it was no small job for just one person. She had done an excellent job – it made the whole kitchen look clean and fresh

Well, after we got home from school and while my mother was preparing dinner, my friend, Grant Smith, and I decided to bounce a rather large ball to each other. One of the foods we were having that night was vegetable soup. Mother had a large bowl of it on the table. The table was located along one wall just on the other side of a doorway that led into our living room.

I don't remember whether Grant bounced the ball in my direction or I bounced it in his, either way, the catch was not made and the ball landed in that large bowl of vegetable soup! The ball – about six inches in diameter, had displaced most of the soup in the bowl. The soup that wasn't on the table cloth had splashed onto mom's newly papered kitchen wall. Poor Grant, very embarrassed was he!

As usual, mom handled my errant behavior in a very controlled manner. I believe she said something like, "Boys, you shouldn't have been playing ball in the kitchen." She had told us that before. But after all, Grant was ten or eleven and I was nine – and we were certain that we wouldn't miss a catch. Obviously, we weren't as sure handed as we thought!

Apparently I was something of a slow learner because even after I was old enough to know better, I continued to do things that vexed my mother. Like the night I came home later than I thought my mother would have liked and decided I'd get to my room without her knowing what time I got home. The front door was not locked so there was no problem getting into the house – but, two or three of the steps on the stairway that led to our upstairs squeaked pretty badly when stepped on. I knew that mom would hear those squeaky stair steps. Besides, I had a better idea. I would climb up on the roof and enter a bedroom window! That should not be too difficult. My little brother's wagon was close by – and there were several cinder blocks close to the back porch. I would be able to put a couple of those blocks in his wagon, climb up on them, and then pull myself to the roof and walk to the window, open it, crawl through the open window and mom would never know what time I got home.

I put the blocks in the wagon, pulled the wagon into the right location, climbed up on the blocks and then secured a good grip with my hands on the edge of the roof. I was all set. With a slight jump, and a strong pull with my arms, presto, my torso is on the roof. However, just at this moment of triumph, the window opens, and a voice says, "Is that you, Billy?" "Yes, mom." "Well, what are you doing?" I didn't answer. I dropped to the ground, went around to the door, opened it and walked up the steps – yes, I stepped on the squeaky ones, too. I went to bed feeling pretty guilty and foolish.

My Sisters' Tormenter

Two of my sisters should have been recognized as having superb control of their emotions and temperament for not conspiring to some how or other exterminate me.(Maybe they did – I just never knew about it!) There was the Saturday morning when I made my oldest sister jump faster than anyone who knew her could ever have imagined.

In our kitchen at that time we had a big black wood stove and there was a stove poker lying on top of it. My sister, Alta, hadn't been out of bed too long and probably wasn't too alert. She was standing on the opposite side of the stove from me – and I saw the poker on the back of the stove with the "business" end on one of the stove plates directly over the fire. The other end of the poker – the hand end was far enough from the plate not to be so hot – but it was very close to me. I can't explain why I did it, but I slowly pushed that poker closer and closer to my sister's rear end until contact was made – but only for the briefest of time. That's when she jumped. And did she jump! Of course, I was smart enough not to linger in the kitchen. I ran for the door, opened it, and in one or two leaps I was off the porch and gone – there was no way she could catch me. Fortunately for me she was more tolerant and more forgiving to me than I deserved – no repercussions.

There were a couple other incidents involving my oldest sister and me. Once, at my grandfather's farm in front of the wagon shed – there was a post hole digger lying on the ground. I was not more than 6 years old and out of the blue, she bet me I could not lift it! We were standing on opposite sides of it and I immediately accepted the bet. I reached down and picked it up and promptly dropped it – it rolled over on her bare toes!!!! I'm certain it hurt, but did it hurt as much as she pretended? I still believe she was a good little actress!

Then, there was another time, also at my grandfather's place, where she and I were sled riding. She was directly ahead of me and must have slid forward on her sled as it started down the hill which forced the rear tips of the runners up in the air. The ends of the runners were not curved as most are today – they were straight and sharp on the end. When the rear end of her sled tipped up, my forehead very near the eye, hit one of the runners – I had a head cut close to the eye which bled profusely and looked much worse than it really was. I am certain our mother was very frightened when she saw the blood and how close the cut was to my eye. Perhaps she scolded my older sister, because she still claims that she got blamed for the accident! She shouldn't have been scolded – my injury wasn't her fault!

There is no question, though, who was to blame the day I loaded my BB gun with sorghum – little seeds I gathered from sorghum growing in a nearby field, and took a couple shots at her rear end when she was some distance from me. I didn't think it would hurt very much – but she did!

Sister Agnes and I

Agnes – Aggie, my youngest sister at the time – about two and a half years younger than I, sometimes teamed up with my older sister and they would raid my cache of hidden apples – they were large pound apples, that I would gather from a tree in our yard. I would squirrel them away in a trunk in which I kept a lot of my valuables – such as, arrow heads, ball bearings, old valentines, or whatever struck my fancy.

They also helped themselves to my bottles of soft drink extracts that I would attempt to hide in a rather large vase – which incidentally, I cracked the bottom of when I dropped the extract bottles into it.

Yes, even the bottled root beer we made that I hid in a garner of wheat was not safe when they started looking for my hidden treasures!!! However, I did get some minor satisfaction when I found I could pick the lock on Alta's small cedar chest with a small nail to possibly find a stick of gum in it!

Aggie sometimes got me into some trouble with our parents – they tended to believe her when we had a dispute over something. However, one day the two of us were on the front porch, alone, when we evidently had some disagreement. A broom was nearby and she picked it up and hit me with it. She then ran inside the house and locked the door. As soon as she ran inside the house and looked back at me through the kitchen door window, she saw me lying on the porch floor going through all kinds of gyrations – She thought she had really hurt me when she hit me, she hadn't! Her kind hearted instincts took control and she opened the door and came out to see what harm she had caused. However, the moment she was away from the door I jumped up, ran inside the house and locked her out – probably until our parents came home!

As a kid I nearly always went bare footed in the summer. I had plenty of scars on my feet to prove it, too! One afternoon my sister, Aggie, and I were in the back yard. There was a small sour cherry tree there and I had a step ladder that I was going to set up against it and then we could climb to the first branch. I lifted the ladder up and as I set it down the foot of the ladder, somehow or other, got caught on the nail of my big toe and tore it off. Believe me, I was in genuine pain – jumping up and down, probably moaning a lot – but my sister thought I was "just acting silly" – She was laughing; enjoying the antics I was performing – little did she know how painful it was to have a toenail torn off. Especially since that toe was already sore from my having dropped the front of a toy wagon on it the week before! She still laughs about it – I still remember the pain!!!!!

Nor did I stop my tormenting when Aggie started to high school. She tells me that I reset her alarm clock to go off at two o'clock in the morning – changing the time that she had set, which was seven. She wondered why the radio programs that she listened to at seven o'clock were not on! It was then she discovered that someone had changed her alarm setting!

And, I just can't believe that I was guilty of raiding the lunch that she had packed for school. She accuses me of taking what she had placed between the slices of bread and replacing it with slices of raw meat! She didn't discover the exchange until she was about to eat lunch the next day with her friends!!! How embarrassing that must have been for her!

In my own defense – if such is possible, none of my pranks or antics were ever done with any thought of malice. The real truth is I would have done anything – still would, for my siblings. Actually all members of my family got along rather well – despite the little squabbles that we often had.

Agnes and I Sell Seeds

There was that day in the spring of the year when Aggie and I left the house to sell seeds. It would be a rather long trek by the time our sales day ended. Before the day was over we would be stopping at Ed Leasure's house and Mandy Smith's house – making our sales pitch to them, hoping they would buy a pack or two of seeds. Those prizes for selling seeds looked so very tempting in the brochure that came with the seed order! We were highly motivated.

Mr. and Mrs. Leasure lived in an old, unpainted house on a steep hillside. Mandy Smith's house was also unpainted, with a rather high front porch that looked out over a meadow that lay alongside of Sideling Hill Creek. We didn't sell many packs, if any, that day. Mrs. Leisure (Cora) looked at a few packs of flower seeds, but she didn't buy. I don't recall what Mandy's preference was, but it was very evident that as a nine and six year old we weren't very dynamic salespeople!

I knew Mandy very well. She often came to my grandfather's store and would always visit in the house for a while. Each time she would see me in his store or his home, she'd always say, "Goodness, how you've grown" It didn't matter if she saw me twice in the same week, she always commented on my growth!

Mandy's maiden name was Barnes. She was a direct descendant of the original Barnes family that had settled in the Gap in the late 1700's. Ed Leasure was also a direct descendant of the original Barnes family. Mandy's father, George, was a sister to Ed's mother, Anne Barnes Leasure.

I remember quite well going with my mother to visit Mrs. Anne Leasure. She was very elderly, lived alone, and was in ill health. My mother would take her food. It seems that someone had taken Mrs. Leasure a pie on a paper plate. She commented on how good the pie was, but the crust was too tough. She ate the plate!

Mr. George Barnes, Mandy's father, was a very old man when I was a boy. His hair was white and he had a long, white beard. My young sister, Aggie, upon seeing George Barnes walk by my grandfather's house told our mother that she had seen Jesus walk by! Those who knew Mr. Barnes were certain that my little sister was wrong.

After Mr. Barnes died there was an estate sale. My mother bought one of the beds sold. A spindle bed, with a rope support for a mattress. The bed was made locally from the black walnut trees that grew in the vicinity. Mother painted it a lettuce green color and put little rose decals on the head and foot boards. It was very attractive. She used a feather stuffed mattress on it. I slept in that little bed for many years as a boy. Later I removed the green paint and refinished it to its original walnut. I still have the bed in my house.

The George Barnes bed with a
"Wedding Ring" cover made by my mother

Our sales route on this day took us up "around the rocks" – today the road has a name, Silver Mills, and it is hard surfaced. The road intersected the main road that ran between the house and barn on my grandfather's place. The intersection with Silver Mills Road was less than a quarter miles from my grandfather's house. The road we were traveling went around the base of the mountain called Rays Hill or Town Hill – the rocks on our right were huge – some were outcrops, others were huge boulders that had not tumbled any further down the side of the mountain. I used to crawl up among those rocks and look for caves. I never found any; only places that seemed to be dug out a bit to provide temporary shelter for foxes, rabbits, or whatever animals that might have been in the area. It also provided a spot for me to look for rocks that might be different from others I had seen. I found rocks that seemed to have a thin, black layer of a different type sandwiched between what was apparently a sedimentary rock.

On occasion I found small stones that had iron pyrites – fools gold, in them. I fully expected to find a "real" nugget of gold in those rocks! Along the bank of that same road I remember seeing what looked like sheets of red rocks. Out croppings of red shale is quite common in that part of Pennsylvania's Ridge and Valley section.

The High Power Rifle Cartridge

Somewhere on that road "around the rocks" we found a .30 .30 caliber rifle cartridge. I put it in my pocket thinking I'd give it to one of my uncles who had a gun of that caliber. Our seed sales were nil and we were getting tired – so we walked a rather long distance to our home.

When we got home I remembered the .30 .30 cartridge in my pocket. I don't know where the idea came from, but suddenly I decided that I'd try to explode it. I found the small single bit axe I owned and placed the shell on a flat stepping stone that was directly in front of our porch steps. My little sister, Aggie, stood right beside me. With the poll end of the axe I struck the cartridge – nothing happened, I struck it again, this time harder. There was a bang, and I felt the force on the axe handle I had in my right hand. The bullet projected only a few inches from where the cartridge had been struck. The casing of the cartridge, however, was nowhere to be found. A year of so later I did find it – it was quite jagged – apparently it had been thrown in a lateral direction and landed underneath our open porch! One or both of us could have been seriously injured if we had been struck by this errant shell casing.

My Umbrella Flight

I was in the third grade and on Friday afternoon I remember reading what I thought was an extremely interesting story. I read it in one of the "readers" that was intended for a fourth or fifth grader – the book was on a shelf with other school textbooks that were probably no longer in use. I recall paging through the book and seeing a drawing of two figures flying over water. The story was about Daedalus and Icarus.

As I remember the story, Daedalus, a very skilled inventor, had come into disfavor with his king. As punishment Daedalus and his son were imprisoned in a labyrinth Daedalus had built for the king. Since Daedalus had built the labyrinth he and his son were able to escape. Daedalus was imprisoned on the island of Crete, but was not permitted to leave by ship. Each day he observed and envied the birds that flew over head – they landed and left the island at will.

His solution to escaping from the island, he thought, was to build a pair of wings for himself and his son. He collected feathers – large and small, and fashioned them into the shape of wings. All surfaces of the wings were filled in smoothly with small feathers. The smooth feathers were given a coating of wax. Daedalus practiced using the invented wings until he could fly. He then taught is son how to fly – but warned him never to fly too high or he might anger the sun god and the wax that was holding the feathers together would melt and he would fall into the sea and drown. He warned him, also, not to fly too close to the sea or the spray would damage his wings – and he would fall into the water. The two decided to escape the island by flying over the sea to another land area.

Icarius, however, was young and found flying very exhilarating – soon he was flying higher and higher. His father was correct – the heat from the sun started melting the wax holding the feathers together and the wings of Icarius began to fall apart. Icarius fell into the sea and drowned. A very saddened Daedalus continued his escape from the island.

On this Saturday morning I was walking toward the barn – Turkey vultures were soaring high overhead in what appeared to me such an effortless way. How I envied the way they were soaring in giant circles so far above me. I was reminded of the story I had read the day before of Daedalus and Icarius. I wondered – could I make a pair of wings? I would need a frame of some sort on which I could glue or attach feathers – Feathers would be no problem, I'd get them from our chicken house. Might have to pluck a chicken or two – or maybe I could use the feathers from a pillow that I knew we had in the house. I could use paraffin wax to hold the feathers together. My mother always had wax – she used it to seal the tops of the jelly jars. She would melt the wax and pour it over the jelly that she had put into the jar – allowing space for the paraffin wax and then she'd screw on the lid.

My real challenge was to find poultry wire fencing with a mesh small enough to hold the feathers. I searched and searched, but I found no poultry fencing with mesh small enough for my project. But, that morning I still wanted to experience flight!

I was some distance below our barn and I looked back at it. The barn was situated on a rather steep hill. The barn floor was considerably higher above the ground at the rear of the barn than it was in front. There was a large door that opened from the back of the barn floor. I never did understand why it was such a large opening – it was used only once a year during the threshing season when the threshing machine was in the barn and a straw stack was wanted outside below the barn. The blower of the thresher would be thrust through the opening and the straw could be directed to a stack below.

As I looked at the opening I began to think of another way I might be able to "fly" that morning. There was a small straw stack a few feet from the wall of the barn – probably no more than three feet high. It had been much higher a year ago, but the rain, snow, and cattle had packed it down until it was no longer much of a stack. Could I, I wondered, jump from that opening holding a large umbrella overhead and float across the small ravine below the barn and land in the field some two – three hundred feet from the jumping off spot? The more I thought about it the more certain I was that I could do it!

Now all I had to do was go back to the house and find the umbrella we had and take my first flight. I searched for the umbrella – finally found it, not in the house, but in a corner with other useless items in a building we called the granary. It hadn't been used for years and it wasn't nearly as large as I envisioned it to be, nor was it in the best physical shape. But I was certain that it would allow me to float through the air for at least a couple hundred feet – maybe more!

I went back to the barn, entered through the barn door, and walked across the floor to the opening overlooking the field where I anticipated my landing. Should I run and jump or should I just jump from the edge of the opening? I opted to just stand and jump as far forward as possible – counting on the umbrella to support my body on my gentle float across the ravine to the field on the other side of it!

No witnesses to record this flight – my preparations had been made without my sisters knowing about it – and certainly my mother didn't know. I had been able to find the umbrella without her knowing. She wasn't very adventurous – she would've nixed the idea in its infancy!

Okay, I'm almost ready. I opened the umbrella, stood on the edge of the opening looking at the field where I anticipated making my landing. With as strong a leap as my eight year old legs would permit, I jumped. Did I float gently over the ravine into the field beyond? No, not at all – I landed on my rear end in the compressed straw below me. One side of the umbrella had folded upward. The flight was a total failure. – taking no more than a couple seconds. I dropped; I didn't float. Fortunately, no broken bones – thank God for the remnants of the straw stack! Thus ended my attempt to emulate the accomplishment of Daedalus and Icarus or to equal the grace that I had admired earlier in the morning of those turkey vultures soaring far overhead. My first flight would have to be delayed many, many years – and it wouldn't be with a pair of home made wings or a flimsy umbrella! Perhaps the lesson that should have been learned then – but hasn't been even after seventy years – I wasn't as smart as I thought I was!

My umbrella flight took off from here

An Early Morning Horse Ride

It was a chilly, but very sunny morning in late winter and I was attending to a chore that I regularly did on non school days – I was watering the two horses that we had in the barn. The horses belonged to my grandfather, but we had two horse stalls in the barn that were not used so we were wintering them. Normally, I just led them to a spring a short distance below the barn and allowed each to drink and then led them back to the barn. They went into their stalls, I put some hay into their mangers, some dry feed into the appropriate dry feed box for each and my chore was done for the morning.

This morning, however, was different. I decided to put a bridle on both horses, climb on the back of the one named Don, and ride up to the house, leading the other horse, a young, rather docile mare, named Bess so that my little sister, Jerri, could see the horses and, more importantly, see me riding one. I was eleven or twelve years old and Jerri was just a toddler – less than two years. Don was a rather high spirited horse who was feeling especially energetic this morning – he hadn't exercised for a while; it was cold and he probably felt that he had a free "rein" with me on his back.

He walked at a pretty brisk pace up to the house. I was sitting up very straight with the lead for the other horse in my left hand. Jerri could see me through thc window in the front door. She was probably in a high chair. I waved to her and in an instant Don and Bess wheeled and started running toward the barn galloping at a much faster speed than I ever wanted or expected. The leather strap that I had in my hand to lead Bess was released and was dangling from her bridle, the docile mare was now just as energetic and frisky as her partner, Don.

The horses were running down a rather steep grade – I couldn't pull back on Don's reins without pulling myself up over his neck! All I could do was cling to his mane and hope for the best! The horses ran by the barn and continued down the hill toward the spring – I was barely holding on, in fact, just before the two horses ran by the spring – they weren't interested in drinking at this point, I went over the head of Don and landed on my side. From where I was lying I could see the two jump the small gully and continue their run into the next field. They circled back and went into the barn, entered their stalls, and to this kid, at least, seemed to be pretty happy with their morning exercise. At this moment I didn't really care if they ever got a drink! I got up, walked to the barn and closed the door to their stalls – I didn't bother removing their bridles – and went back to the house feeling as though I'd been "thrown from a horse." I don't believe my little sister ever realized how scared her big brother was that morning – just to let her see those horses with me riding one of them.

Smoking a Cigar

I was on my way home from baseball practice. I had ridden my bicycle to the practice field about four miles away; it was across the road from Ritz Brother's store – a general store that was patronized by the local farmers. It was a well stocked rural store carrying animal feeds, various hardware that would be used on the farm, canned goods, other household staples, and in general, many items that patrons would otherwise have to drive to Hancock, Maryland to purchase – roughly twenty miles away.

I left the practice field and rode my bike toward home. It was about three o'clock in the afternoon when I was within about a mile of my parent's house. In my shirt pocket I had a cigar that someone had given to me. I wasn't a smoker. Oh, yes, I had made a few little pipes out of acorns and tried smoking corn silk, but I found that to be too bitter and certainly, nothing to try more than once! Also, one evening after I got off the school bus – I had a mile to walk to my home, I tried smoking a cigarette. My science teacher was admonishing the entire class not to smoke – he proceeded to tell us how the burning tars would coat the lining of our lungs and eventually harm our health. (Apparently he didn't practice what he preached – he was known to go to the furnace room during the school day for a smoke!) His proof of the tar residue was to tell us that if we blew cigarette smoke through a white handkerchief it would leave a yellowish stain on the handkerchief.

One of my smoking friends had given me a cigarette – which I carried in my pocket, along with a pack of book matches. No one else was walking home with me that afternoon after I got off the school bus so I lit the cigarette and proceeded to blow smoke through the handkerchief. Sure enough, there was a yellow stain on it. I inhaled a few times and decided I didn't like it – besides, I had begun to feel a bit nauseous. I tossed the cigarette to the road, stepped on it to make certain it was out and went home.

On my last mile from baseball practice before reaching my parents' house, was a steep hill – too steep for me to pedal my bike so I had to push it up this hill. However, after getting to the top I could ride the rest of the way home. Not very far from the top of the hill was an old apple orchard on the left side of the road—many of the trees had died, but quite a number of them still stood. One of my favorite trees was one that still produced fruit – an old variety called, "Sweet Paradise." Many times in late September when walking home from school I would stop and eat an apple that had fallen from this tree.

As I rode my bicycle by the orchard I suddenly thought of the cigar that I had in my pocket. It was a hot day in late July and the shade from the Sweet Paradise tree looked very inviting. I was still a bit tired from pushing the bicycle up the steep hill and I was perspiring. I stopped my bike, pushed it under the lower strand of the barb wire fence and sat down under the apple tree. I leaned my back against the tree trunk and said to myself, "Now is a good time to smoke that cigar." I removed the wrapper, bit off the end – I had seen cigar smokers do that – but I guess I didn't know why, "Which end do I put in my mouth," I thought? I made the decision to put the cut end in my mouth and then proceeded to light the other end. In an instant, it seemed, I was puffing bluish white smoke into the atmosphere! I decided to inhale – after some initial coughing, I was able to inhale and even blew smoke through my nose.

After only a few minutes of this I noticed the trees in the orchard appeared to be moving around me! And, I had a nauseous feeling in my stomach. Better get on home, I thought, besides I'd had enough of the cigar. I had smoked about three quarters of it. I pushed the lighted end into the ground and started to get up. But I could barely stand. I held onto the tree trunk that I had been resting my back against and those trees in the orchard were really spinning around me, now!

Somehow or other I got my bicycle under the lower strand of the barbed wire fence and out onto the road. I tried riding it but my balance was completely gone. I was only about two tenths of a mile from my home so I had a choice – leave it alongside of the road and walk home, or push the bike. I opted to push it.

By now I had what some of my friends would call the "dry heaves"! I wanted the worst way to vomit – but there was nothing in my stomach to come out – so every minute or so it seemed, I'd go through one of these episodes of trying to up-chuck! At last, I pushed the bicycle into the driveway of my home. Now what shall I do? I didn't want my mother to know what I had done; I couldn't go into the house, either. I laid the bike down and walked around to the back of the house and threw myself down on the grass. I still had those "dry heaves" and so sick that I really didn't care if I lived another minute! My mother probably heard me in what must have sounded to her like my death throes, – suddenly, she came around the corner of the house and looked at me and said, "What in the world is wrong with you?"

"I'm sick," I said. I don't believe I needed to say that, my appearance spoke louder than anything that I could have said. Her next question was what any mother would have asked, "What made you sick?" I guess I still wasn't certain I would not die, so a good time for a deathbed confession. "I smoked a cigar, Mom." I think she was probably relieved that there was not something more seriously wrong with me.

As I remember she said something like you'll feel better after while – just don't smoke any more cigars and went back into the house. She was correct – in another hour I did feel much better.

Actually, in retrospect, the cigar smoking incident was probably a very good thing for me. I never wanted to smoke after that – even while in the military where it seemed everyone smoked cigarettes, I was never even tempted. After all, in the mind of a fourteen year old who was pretty certain he was not going to survive the consequences of his first cigar – a strong lesson had been learned.

A Night Visit to the Buck Valley Tomato Cannery

It was pretty much a regular baseball practice. Those of us who played had gone to the practice field at Ritz Brothers' store – it was a nice practice field, complete with bleachers behind the catcher – screened, of course, to protect the spectators – assuming we had any, from fowl balls and errant throws from the not too proficient players – of which we had nine!

I didn't ride my bicycle that evening; instead, my cousin, Homer Fischer, who was 16, and had his driver's license, drove his dad's car. He lived about a mile from where I did so he asked me to ride along with him. And I was quite happy to do that. Typically, we would practice until it was nearly dark and then go up to the store – which was only a few hundred feet from the ball diamond, and have a soft drink, a candy bar and just "talk," then we'd go home. Tonight, however, was a little different. Homer had a car! Someone said, "Let's go over to the tomato cannery." the cannery was a local operation, no more than a couple miles from where we were. In late summer and early fall local farmers brought tomatoes to the cannery and sold them. The tomatoes were marketed under the name of "Buck Valley Brand Tomatoes".

One year I set out an acre of tomato plants, picked the ripe tomatoes in ½ bushel containers and sold them to the cannery. Local farm wives would work there during the season peeling tomatoes – or whatever else that had to be done. A few men worked there, also – firing the boiler, heavy lifting, and managing the work force. My mother worked there at times, not every season, but I remember her working there a few summers during the canning season.

About six of us got into Homer's car. In a few minutes we were there. I should have known that we weren't just going there to see how tomatoes were canned! It was only a matter of seconds until someone got the idea to snatch a half bushel of tomatoes and bombard the cannery. There were ample targets – windows were open, no screens or glass, and real live targets just inside those windows. Plus, there were a couple men outside that would be within range of a lobbed, juicy tomato. I don't recall who snatched the half bushel of tomatoes and brought it back to where the tomatoes would be used as missiles – but we were far enough away that the rather dim light of the cannery probably protected us from being recognized.

Somebody in our group threw the first tomato – aimed, I think at one of the open windows. It missed but the "plop" of the impact was easily heard. Soon the red missiles were flying – one of my ball player friends, shouted, "I got him." Others may have scored direct hits as well, but there was not time to relish the accuracy!

I saw this man coming – I knew him and a nicer person never lived. But, from what he was saying and the speed at which he was moving in our direction, told everyone that his was not a welcoming speech! Perhaps my partners knew the location better than I did – they disappeared very quickly. I tried moving out of range, certainly eyesight of the man coming in my direction – but, I hadn't moved more than five or ten feet until I was against a fence. I was in a thicket of briars, underbrush, and I didn't know what else. I made it over the fence and threw myself down in the middle of briars and all sorts of underbrush. The man who was headed in our direction continued – I could hear him plainly now. He was still walking and talking when he came to where I had been standing just a few seconds ago. Gosh, I thought, Can he see me here? Will he continue moving toward me? Will he say, "Hey you, yes, you lying in those briars, I know who you are, come out of there." But, he stopped his forward movement and appeared to have finished his discourse. Maybe he ran out of words or perhaps in his wisdom he knew that all of us had heard him and we would not be throwing anymore tomatoes! But, I didn't think I was in the clear yet. Had he seen me. He knew me, he knew my parents – what will they say when he tells them about this incident. Could I be arrested for this caper, I wondered? One of my teachers has some kind of financial interest in this cannery – what will he think of me? My conscience was in overdrive now – where was it before I got into this mess??? In a few minutes my friends and I reassembled, got into Homer's car, and left! Well, as far as I know none of us suffered any repercussions from the evening. But, I'll never know if Mr. Beatty saw that scared 14 year old buried in the briars barely ten feet from him!!

I did tell my parents. They weren't very pleased when I told them about the episode – but, they really didn't have to scold. That minute of so that I was within a few feet of Mr. Beatty re-awakened my conscience! I'd like to believe that future episodes of that nature were avoided because "Conscience" spoke before I got myself into trouble.

Exploring Our Nearby Woods

With a woods in my backyard to explore, a couple streams in which to swim and fish and a great imagination to foster excitement – I had a very good life in the boonies! I had the opportunity to live the life of Huckleberry Finn and Tom Sawyer! I enjoyed climbing the young hickory trees in the woods below our house. When I was near the top of one I'd swing my body away from the tree and it would bend nearly to the ground! Once in a while the sapling would break and I'd hit the ground a little harder than I wanted to, but that only added to the excitement!

One of the trails I often followed took me by a couple large persimmon trees. In the fall of the year they were usually loaded with the small orange fruit. After a couple hard frosts some of the persimmons were edible. Persimmons do not all ripen at the same time – so the period that one would find edible persimmons extended over a rather long time span. A fully ripe persimmon is extremely soft and usually falls from the tree at this ultra ripe stage. The very soft, ripe fruit is extremely sweet. However, if one makes a mistake and eats one that is not completely ripe – the lips feel as though they may have gone into a permanent "pucker." The unripe fruit is extremely astringent because of the tannin it contains. The tannin apparently is not present in the fully ripe persimmon.

On this same trail I remember the wild pussy willow bush in the spring time. I could cut off some of the branches, take them home or to school, put them into a vase of water and in a few days the buds would be in full bloom.

I knew where to find the June berry trees, too, sometimes called Service berry or Shadbush. In the latter part of May, sometimes early June these little trees would produce a rather large crop of small, waxy, sweet, red berries that actually turn to a dark purple when fully ripe. Usually I didn't have to climb the tree to get to the berries. I could reach the lower branches and pull them down to strip the berries off them. I was always in competition with the birds, though, they knew where these small tree grew, also – and they would visit them very early in the morning, before I was out of bed.

Years later I would learn that the June berry tree belongs to the rose family. Other than eating them off the tree we did nothing else with them. Perhaps because the birds were much more aggressive in picking them than my family was.

I also knew where to find those very large fox grapes that had a wonderful fragrance. They had a flavor very much like a Concord grape, of course, they were much larger and had a thicker skin. In late September I knew where to find vines that produced somewhat small cluster of these large blue black grapes. My mother would often make juice or jelly from them.

Sometime during the latter part of June I would look for blackberries – the high ones and those that grew on vines that hugged the ground on rather poor ground that was currently not being cultivated – sometimes called dewberries, but we always called them blackberries. The little cluster of berries were well protected by the many thorns or spines that were on the vines. In the process of picking the hands would always be scratched! The berries of the high variety were a bit sweeter, I thought, and somewhat easier to pick. I could pick them while standing upright; in picking the trailing ones I had to bend over. Sometimes my mother and sisters would also pick them. We'd take our buckets and pick until the berries were gone or our buckets were full! My mother would make jelly or jam from them. I always preferred the jam, even though there were many seeds in it! I picked the little huckleberries, too, but I didn't like to do that. On the little bushes were tiny mite larvae, called chiggers, that would burrow into the skin under the belt or any place where the clothing was tight and cause little red, itchy welts to appear that would result in my scratching them.

Also, in our woods I would search out the little teaberry plants and eat not only the little red berry that might be underneath the leaves, but also chew the leaves. They had a very strong wintergreen flavor. In the spring of the year in the same location where the teaberry plants grew, there was always a forest floor covering of Trailing Arbutus. They were beautiful, dainty little flowers with a wonderful fragrance! I remember the morning I found a beautiful yellow flower at the base of a rather large tree. It was a Moccasin flower, the first I had ever seen.

In May and the early part of June there were many wild honey suckle bushes in bloom in the woods. I loved the pink to reddish colors of the flowers. Also, along the road that ran by our house the little wild roses, both pink and white, grew abundantly during the spring and early summer. Later in the summer I would see the bright orange blossom of the orange milkweed.

While on these treks I would locate and gather pine knots. We used the pine knots as kindling to start the fire in our wood burning stoves. I'd split them with an axe into pieces maybe one half to an inch in diameter – it would take only a few splints to get a fire started in the stove each morning. The pine knots that I gathered were from large yellow pines that had blown down or died many years ago.. The knot – which was where a branch of the tree had been attached to the main trunk, was very slow to decay. Over time most of the tree, excepting the knots and parts of the root, would decay. The knots and part of the roots contained a large concentration of resin or pitch. The resin made the knot impervious to moisture. Sometimes they were almost completely covered with decayed leaves. I recall being able to pick up many pine knots just by moving in a straight line along the path that the tree had fallen. Some of the roots of the stump were also rich in resin and we used that to start our fires, too.

Our pioneer ancestors also used pine knots – not just for starting fires, but for lighting purposes. A splint of pine could be inserted into a holder and placed in the fireplace and it would provide enough light to do some household work. The fireplace had to be used because burning the resin rich pine produced a great deal of rather pungent smoke. In some areas of the country wood kindling cut from pine knots was referred to as "fat wood."

I was particularly fond of my romps in a certain section of land on my grandfather's farm. Along a small spring fed run in a heavily wooded area there was a beautifully shaped hemlock tree. At the time I believed it to be an ancient tree! I would go there alone and fantasize that many years before me some Indian children probably visited the same spot. I convinced myself that I was probably standing exactly where some Indian boy about my age had once stood! I realized much later in life that this hemlock was probably not over 50 or 75 years old. Because of its location it had plenty of moisture and had not been attacked by any harmful insects; it was able to make very fast growth. In my mind's eye I can still see that beautiful Hemlock tree.

Finding Two Indian Graves

My interest in Indians led me to believe for several years that two rows of stones about ten feet long covered two Indian graves! My friend, James Shanholtz, pointed to the two rows of stones one time when we passed them while taking a short cut through the woods to school. He told me they were Indian graves and that the Indians buried their dead in shallow graves and covered them with stones to keep wild animals from disturbing them. James was a couple years older than I was and spoke with authority – the story sounded plausible, and I believed it one hundred percent. I continued to believe it until one day a year or so later I was describing something I had seen to an uncle and I referenced the location as being close to the Indian graves. You can believe his ears perked up when I said Indian graves! When I described the location of the two "graves" he laughed and explained that his father and his uncle had gathered the stones from a nearby field and had piled them inside the woods where they wouldn't interfere with farming that field.

Those two rows of stones were put there by my grandfather and my great Uncle George only twenty or twenty five years before James and I discovered them – not the one hundred years plus that we thought. Yet, that mistaken belief served a positive purpose: It permitted me to fantasize for a couple of years about the Indian artifacts that might be buried in those "graves"!

Rolling Tires down the Face of the Mountain

The face of the mountain behind grandfather's farm house had been cleared of trees and underbrush. Sheep and cattle used to graze there. A cousin and I used to take automobile tires part way up the face of the mountain and let them roll down the side. There was a small spring fed run at the foot of the mountain and after a rain it would be flowing pretty well. The tires that we rolled down the mountain would gain considerable speed and momentum before leaping the small run and crashing into the fence that had been built to keep the live stock from leaving their mountain side enclosure. Obviously, our grandfather and uncles weren't very happy about the tires damaging the fence when they would crash into it. Sometimes we would load rather heavy stones inside the tire – by the time the tire had reached the lower part of its run, it was literally leaping! Thank goodness we were never successful when we attempted to fit ourselves inside the tire and roll down the mountainside!!!

On the top of this mountain face was a flat surface. Years ago it had apparently been cultivated. When I was a boy there were some old pear trees still producing fruit on top of the mountain. In the fall of year the pears were hauled down the side of the mountain loaded on a sledge – (a sled with heavy wooden runners that was used by farmers before wagons were widely utilized) A wagon could not be used at this site – its speed could not be controlled down the mountain side. I remember eating pears from those old trees.

Big Little Books

I thoroughly enjoyed reading Big Little Books. I bought them for ten cents a piece. The format used in the books was quite simple – one page of text; one page of line drawings. The titles of books and topics covered ranged from comic strip adventures and their characters to historical events and their heroes. Many of the books had western heroes and adventures. I had a couple that featured Dick Tracey and his detective prowess – another detective, Dan Dunn, was also a Big Little Book hero. One of my favorite Big Little Books was about Kit Carson, the Indian scout.

When my family would drive to Hancock, Maryland to shop, I'd go to the five and dime store and look over the selection of Big Little Books. I would decide on one, buy it, and then head back to the car and start reading. My mother would say to me before we got home, "Why don't you just read part of it now and save the rest until later?" But, I didn't want to do that – I couldn't stop reading until I had turned the last page! I remember, too, the Better Little Books, I believe they superceded the Big Little Books.

Great literature they weren't, but for an hour or so, each one that I owned certainly held my attention. I still don't know what happened to my collection of these little books. By the time I was about 15 I had quite a collection of them. My parents had a trash pile in the "pines" – I suspect that after I left home those Big Little Books got carted to the trash pile! Wish I still had them.

My Reading Retreat

There was a certain place on our farm where I kept a cache of reading materials. Across from the house several hundred yards – a bit south of east, there was a large walnut tree. It was at the head of a gully. A short distance below the gully was the beginning of a grove of "scrub pines," we called them. Under a pine tree that was somewhat larger than the others was a rusty sheet of tin roofing. It had probably blown there several years ago when the barn had burned. This large piece of tin made a perfect shelter for magazines, books, and newspapers that I would place there. It was a wonderful place to sit and read – especially in the summer and early fall. A big plus, also, was that it was very close to the field where my dad would plan my work week. He worked away from home for five days and then he would be home for two. The field I am referring to was "growing up," as he put it, with scrub pines and other vegetation that would have precluded its being farmed in the traditional way. My work assignment in that field was always the same – cut the pines off at ground level as well as the other brush that was growing there, uninvited!. Frankly, as a twelve or thirteen year old kid, I doubted if that field would ever grow corn, wheat, or any grain crop again – I preferred seeing it revert back to a forest! Maybe I was just trying to find an acceptable rationalization to justify my not wanting to do the hard work that was required to get rid of what my dad saw as unwanted vegetation. Guess I saw little pleasure in using the axe or that mowing scythe, dad called a brush hook, ours had a very heavy strong blade that made it useful in cutting sturdy brush. I preferred doing other activities! I kept an abundance of reading material under that sheet of rusty tin. And even if I didn't have what I wanted to read stored under my sheet of tin, I would take other reading material to that location and read it. My oldest sister was in high school and occasionally she would bring books home for me to read. One that she brought home was a rather thick book about the

Civil War, titled, *On the Trail of Grant and Lee*. Another that I read in my "retreat" was Eric Remarque's, *All Quiet on the Western Front*. I don't remember where I got it, but I read part of Margaret Mitchell's, *Gone with the Wind* under that pine tree. There were many others as well.

We did not subscribe to them, but friends would give us their out-dated magazines. Many of these I stored underneath the tin sheet of roofing. I remember Colliers, Look, and Life – these were my favorites. I don't remember where they came from, but at times I would have sections of newspapers – The Pittsburgh Gazette, the Cumberland Times, and the Hagerstown Morning Herald under my sheet of tin roofing library.

Many, many years later I revisited my old library. After brushing away a rather thick layer of pine needles I uncovered that old sheet of tin. No, none of my magazines were left but I could see tiny particles of what at one time had been paper – the field mice had made very good use of my reading material

My Inventions

I don't believe I was ever any happier than when I would get a new number 9 dry cell. With a new dry cell and a length of door bell wire I was ready to make everything from electro magnets, electric motors, radios, door bells – but, from a practical standpoint the only thing I ever made that would work was an electro magnet. That was pretty simple – simply wrap a ten penny or larger nail with a few coils of wire, connect the two ends of the wire to the terminals of the dry cell and I had a working, electro magnet. Oh, I believe I did get flash light bulbs to light – I did not realize at first why they burned out so quickly! At some point I figured out that my number 9 dry cell was too powerful for the bulbs I was taking out of our flashlights! My motors never worked – even though I thought I had done everything that was necessary to have the rotor spinning! Guess my brushes weren't positioned correctly – but, a ten year old doesn't always have enough patience to work out problems.

My shortage of patience probably resulted in the failure of my "steam engine" project, too. I had seen a picture of a small steam engine that I thought was a model of the one James Watt had built. Using the same principle that I believed was evident in the drawing I had seen, I found a gallon can, punched a hole near the top of it and inserted a piece of copper tubing about a foot long. I made a small fan out of wood, punched a hole through the center and mounted it in a frame and placed it close to my can. I then bent the copper tubing so that the end of it could exhaust the steam or vapor directly onto the fan. I poured about a half gallon of water into the gallon can, screwed the cap onto the can's opening, built a small fire under the can – and, as soon as the water started to boil I expected to see the water vapor coming out of the copper tubing causing the fan to turn. I don't know what happened, maybe I had too sharp a bend in the tubing – all I know for certain is that after a long time the rectangular shaped can began to take on a rounded appearance and the fan was not rotating – in fact, nothing was coming out of the tubing! The heck with this, I thought, my patience had been exhausted. I picked up a stone and threw it into the side of the can. The stone punctured the side of the can and the steam shot out towards me! Fortunately, I was far enough away not to get scalded. Another failure!!!!

I tried making playable musical horns out of the large, hollow, leaf stems of the squash plant. By cutting off the stem near the ground and then removing the leaf at the other end, I would make a small slit in the top of the stem with my pocketknife just at the point where I had cut off the leaf – there is a natural depression at this location. By putting the split end of the squash stem in my mouth and blowing through it, the slit would vibrate and make a horn sound. The larger the stem diameter and the longer the stem, the deeper the sound. So, I reasoned that if I punched holes in the top of the stem and held my fingers over those holes – then released a finger—I thought I could control the pitch, thus, able to play a tune! Theoretically, I still believe my plan should have worked. Maybe my "pucker" wasn't just right, maybe I didn't blow hard enough – whatever the reason, another failure!!!

My failures, though, didn't deter me from trying to make other types of "toys" that would work. I loved tearing old alarm clocks apart and attempting to harness the spring power to move some crude toys I tried making out of wood. Actually, I did achieve minor successes in this area.. For many years after my experiments, one could still see the cog marks on one of the window sills where I had tried out my "clock" toys.

Making Whirly Gig

But, I did have success in making propellers out of wood – whirly gigs, we called them. With a strip of white pine wood, one inch square and about five or six inches long, I would locate the exact center, since I didn't have a drill or brace and bit, I heated an 8 or 9 penny nail until it was red hot and holding it with a pair of pliers I would then burn a hole in the center of what would be the propeller. Next, with a pocket knife I would shave either side of my pine blank at the correct angle, push a nail through the burned hole and, if the wind were blowing hold the propeller above my head to see if it would turn – if no wind was blowing I would run a short distance holding the propeller over my head for a test. If the propeller turned – I'd cut a longer piece of my one inch square stock, find a flat, thin piece of metal and tack it onto the tail end of the strip. I was well on my way to making a workable weather vane! The rest of the job was pretty easy. I had to burn another hole with a red hot nail through the strip so that I could drive a nail through it into an upright standard that I would nail onto a fence post. My weather vane could then pivot depending upon the direction of the wind. Also, with a smaller nail I would make a "pilot" hole in the end of my weather vane strip so that I could drive the nail that would go through the center of my propeller into it. If I didn't burn the pilot hole I risked splitting the end of the wood. Sometimes I tried to be fancy by making a four bladed weather vane instead of the simpler one!.

Making Sling Shots

I made great slingshots, too! I had two styles – one that was forked and one that used only a single stick. The forked one worked much better. Materials for making slingshots were always available and the tools needed were a pocketknife, a pair of pliers and maybe a pair of scissors. I would go to the woods and find a young tree that had a forked branch. With a pocketknife I would cut the main stem and then proceed to trim the two forks until they were the desired lengths. My next step was to find an old automobile or bicycle inner tube and cut two strips to the length I wanted, usually from 8 to 10 inches – the strips were about one half to three quarters of an inch in width. For the pocket of the slingshot I needed to find an old shoe and cut out the tongue. Now, all I needed to do was assemble it! Just below the tip of each fork I would remove about three quarters of an inch of bark, leaving about a quarter inch of bark on the very tip. Then, I'd wrap the end of the rubber strip around the fork where I had removed a section of the bark. With a short piece of copper wire, usually doorbell wire, I would secure the rubber band to the fork. After doing the same thing with the other rubber strip I was ready to secure the leather pocket to the rubber strips. I would shape the shoe tongue to the desired size and punch two holes on either side of it. Next, I would taper the ends of the rubber strips slightly and force them through the holes in the tongue of the pocket. The last step was to double back the rubber strips that I pushed through the holes in my sling pocket and secure them with my bell wire by making several wraps around each just outside the pocket. Now, I was ready to see if I could hit that can that I had set on the post – fifteen feet away!

The one made with a single hand hold was made essentially the same as the forked one – except that both rubber strips were attached to the end of single hand hold. This type didn't work as well as the forked one did. I made this kind only when I couldn't find a suitable fork in one of our trees.

My Gym in the Barn

I don't know why I had this great interest in exercising or trying to acquire a strong body, unless it was because I saw the Charles Atlas ad in so many magazines and comic books that I read. Remember, the ads where the bully kicked sand into the face of the 97 pound weakling??? Additionally, there were the ads that were placed by the York Barbell Company that showed men with admirable physiques. I saw other such ads that featured the Good Brothers and their body building equipment, too. The price of their 160 pound barbell and dumbbell set must have been within my budget, because without informing anybody else in our household I ordered it. A couple weeks later a card came in the mail telling me that it had been delivered to the B&O Freight Office in Hancock, Maryland. I told my dad about it – he had no idea what a barbell was – he had his own conception of what a dumbbell was though. I suspect he thought he was rearing one! Anyway, he took me to the B&O Freight Office in Hancock and I went into the depot to retrieve my shipment. The bar was separate, but everything else, the plates, the dumbbell bars and the instruction books and charts were in a wooden box. I lifted the box onto a low wagon that was in the depot, along with the bar that weighed twenty pounds, and pulled the load to dad's car that was parked nearby. I struggled a bit getting the box into the trunk – my dad helped, "What's in that thing," he said – referencing the box.

"Those are the plates that are used on the barbell," I'm certain he must have thought he had a complete moron for a son, what would anyone do with this five foot bar and a box full of iron plates? I must confess I had never seen a real barbell – other than in magazines! I had made my own facsimile – quite different from what I now had. My home made one was a broom stick with two five gallon buckets on either end partially filled with dirt and stones that I had gathered from the garden and anyplace I could find suitable material. My apparatus was not easy to work with – the weights on either end of the broom stick were not equal, plus the weights had a tendency to either slide off the end or toward the center of my bar.

My home made set was kept behind our garage. However, I took the new set to the barn and immediately had plans for a rather complete gym! There were a couple iron well pipes around the barn, I don't know why they were there, but they were about two inches in diameter and five or six feet in length. On the barn floor there was an opening through which hay was thrown to animals on the lower level. I placed the two iron pipes across this opening and immediately had a place where I could do chin ups and dips.

My dad and a friend had converted part of the barn floor into a chicken enclosure. The top of the chicken enclosure was covered with heavy oak boards. It was easily reached by an eight foot ladder that was attached to the side of their construction. This would be the area where I would work out! In the wooden box with the barbell plates were the instruction books and charts illustrating the various exercises. I tacked the charts on the wall, carried the plates, one by one up the ladder to the top of the chicken enclosure, brought the box up, too. I would use the box for bench pressing and any exercises that I needed to do in a sitting position.

Three days a week I visited my gym. I knew nothing of "warm-up" exercises. I'd go directly to my chinning pipe and suspend myself over the "hay-hole" and begin my work out. (It would have been quite a drop if my hands slipped.) After the chinning exercises I would manipulate the second pipe into a comfortable position and do my dips between the bars. After that, I was ready for the real "work out." I would climb the ladder to where the barbell and dumbbells were and follow the exercise plan suggested in the manual and shown on the charts. I believe I did every exercise shown and discussed on the charts and in the manual. I did the presses, something called a military press, the clean and jerk, deep knee bends with weight on my shoulders – I continued that routine for several weeks. I finally asked myself, "Why are you doing this?" "Did any bully ever kick sand in your face?" The answer, of course, was no! I'd never even been to a beach! Besides, I didn't know any bullies – I'd never been bullied by anyone even though I could have qualified as a 97 pound weakling! Eventually I backed off the rigorous training routine – but, I must admit that since that time I have maintained an interest in regularly exercising – certainly not with the same enthusiasm I had in those adolescent days!

The weights were borrowed a couple times by friends, and the borrowers would often forget to return them. But I always managed to retrieve them somehow. I still have the complete set, but their use has certainly waned in the past sixty years!

Chapter 5

Barnes's Gap School

Description

I attended Barnes Gap elementary for seven years. It was not unlike the other one room schools in the area. There were eight grades – the number of students in each grade ranged from two or three to maybe as many as six. The total school enrollment during any one school term that I attended did not number more than twenty one students. The inside of the school was pretty bare. A board floor, was oiled once or twice a year to keep down dust. There was a bank of large window on either side protected on the outside by a heavy chain like wire screen, plus there were two window in the front that faced the porch. The structure was heated by a rather large wood burning stove with a smoke pipe going straight up through the ceiling and then, into a chimney that began above the ceiling, one could see it projecting through the roof of the school building. Several panels of slate covered much of the back wall that served as the chalkboard. Above the chalkboards, in the center of them, was a set of wall maps; each of which was on a roller that the teacher or student could pull down when needed. Oh, yes, there was also that large unfinished portrait of George Washington staring down at us! Facing the students was the teacher's desk, not a large one but a sturdy one made of oak. To the extreme right of the teacher's desk was a cabinet – or cupboard in which books and other school supplies were stored. In the left rear of the room was a pedal organ that was purchased by Miss Shank, my second grade teacher. To the left front of the teacher's desk was the recitation bench!

When the teacher was ready to instruct a certain grade she/he asked pupils to come to the recitation bench. The students would go to the bench that extended from the edge of the center isle to the edge of the side isle and sit down. If it were a spelling class students did not sit down but stood as the teacher pronounced each word for oral spelling. Sometimes the words were not spelled orally, but students remained in their seats and wrote the spelling words on paper – sometimes students had a narrow spelling tablet in which the words were written. At the Barnes Gap school there were corner shelves built into the wall on the extreme left and right of the wall as one came into the school house from the front porch. The water cooler sat on one of the shelves on the left side at the front of the room. It was a stone crock, barrel shaped utensil, grey with some blue stripes running horizontally around it. One secured water from the cooler by holding his glass under the spigot just above the bottom of the water container and pushing inward on the valve of the spigot. Lunch boxes were placed on these shelves, too. Hats and coats were hung on hooks on the wall just inside the door.

There was a rather large front porch at Barnes Gap School. The two ends were enclosed and the front near each end was also enclosed. Wood was stored on the porch; the partial enclosure protected it from rain and snow. During my first couple of years at Barnes's Gap, the school house was unpainted; later it was painted white.

During the winter months the interior of the school room was somewhat cold for the first hour or so – the ceiling was high, there was no insulation in the sides of the building, ceiling, or floor and the single paned windows did not fit too tightly in their frames. Students sometimes sat close to the stove until the room warmed up. Nearly all walked to school – some a distance of two miles. I walked a mile, if I went by road; less than that if I took a shortcut through the fields and woods.

I remember one time it snowed nearly all day. At dismissal time, Ralph Smith, one of the parents arrived at the school with a team of horses, with bells on them, pulling a large bobsled. All of us who lived in the direction of his home climbed aboard and rode as far as we could in our direction on the sled. The ride was a lot of fun!

Pupil Attendance

Interestingly, attendance was very good. Of the seven years I attended I had perfect attendance for five of those years. There was a certificate of Perfect Attendance given the first year of perfect attendance and after the first year a seal was issued by the Department of Public Instruction that was affixed to the certificate. The practice was discontinued at the close of the 1940 school term because someone believed that it encouraged children to attend school when they were ill and should have stayed at home! I was a bit angry because I had perfect attendance in 1941; I drew my own seal on the certificate!!

Commonwealth of Pennsylvania

DEPARTMENT OF PUBLIC INSTRUCTION

CERTIFICATE OF PERFECT ATTENDANCE

This is to certify that William Smith, a pupil in the public schools of the Commonwealth of Pennsylvania, in accordance with a statement filed by the teacher, has been neither absent nor tardy during the school year certified below by the seal of the Department of Public Instruction.

DEPARTMENT OF PUBLIC INSTRUCTION PERFECT ATTENDANCE 1936

DEPARTMENT OF PUBLIC INSTRUCTION PERFECT ATTENDANCE 1939

DEPARTMENT OF PUBLIC INSTRUCTION PERFECT ATTENDANCE 1940

No. 62727

SERIES 15—1936

Superintendent of Schools

Superintendent of Public Instruction

My attendance certificate and seals

All my sibling had excellent school attendance, as well. Our parents would not have had it otherwise. On more than one occasion I recall my dad saying that there were many days when he wanted to go to school but "pap" made him stay home and work on the farm. The attitude displayed by his father was probably not too different from that expressed by many others living in rural areas on small farms. I learned later that not too far from where my dad's father lived was a school district that refused to fund the schools for several years. The Free School Act of 1834 provided for free public schools. Each county was divided into districts and each district could decide if it wanted to participate. The district in Southampton Township in Bedford County agreed to the terms of participation. However, there was a great deal of opposition after accepting the original agreement. In 1857 the school board resigned and for a period lasting until 1866 there were no public schools operating in that district. Many people in the district refused to pay their taxes to support the schools. The schools reopened only after the State intervened and compelled the district to open the schools.. I can't help wondering if my dad's father was not influenced by the same attitude reflected by those a generation earlier, i.e., education was an abstract value that had limited value compared to the immediate value of not paying school taxes and getting the crops into the ground at the proper time! Thank goodness my dad had a much more enlightened attitude toward education for his children than was apparently the case during his childhood.

Other than chicken pox, measles, or other childhood communicable disease of the type that would result in greater than usual absences, all the children appeared to be very healthy and attendance was generally very good. Could the absence of illness be related to the fact that everyone had to walk a considerable distance to and from school, plus the outdoor play experienced during two fifteen minute recess periods and a one hour lunch period?

Outdoor Games Played At School

Only on days when the weather was truly inclement or a child had a severe cold did anyone remain indoors. The outdoor games were adapted to the weather conditions. When snow covered the playground a giant ring was tramped in the snow with numerous path made from the center to the perimeter. A kind of tag was played – when being chased by the person who was "it" the chaser and the chased had to remain on the paths that had been made previously. The objective of the chased was to get back to home base without being tagged – which was the center of the circle. If tagged, you were out of the game! As I remember, though, there were no hard and fast rules for any of the games we played. They could and were often changed!

As indicated above – most of our games were played outdoors. Ball games were always popular. We played a form of baseball – without a baseball, instead we used a "sponge" or rubber ball. Most of the rules of regulation baseball were followed, but we played without fielders' gloves or mitts. And catching a ball on "first bounce" was as legitimate as catching a fly ball! Another ball game we played that differed considerably from our regular "baseball" was one that we called "Double batters" Instead of a single batter and a single pitcher we had two – facing each other. The bases were run as in our regular game, but when a fielder caught a ball on the fly or first bounce, he then replaced that batter and the batter took the fielder's place. Rules for this game were quite flexible and subject to change – depending, I believe, on the size and aggressiveness of the players! A number of different games were played – Crack the Whip was one. I remember playing this game when I was quite small and, I was usually on the very end of the string of persons playing. – which meant I went flying through the air when those at the head of the chain stopped and the sweeping motion of the chain of players continued! Then, there was Annie Over. Two teams on either side of the school building were formed. One person on the team would throw the ball over the building and yell, “Annie Over.” If it were caught the catching team would come running round the building to “tag” members of the other team. If tagged, that player would have to remain with the team that tagged him. Other members of the opposite team attempted to run round the building to the side where the catching team had been. If the ball were not caught, them that team would throw the ball over the building and yell, “Annie Over” and be prepared to race to the other side if they saw members of the opposite team coming round the building to tag them. The game continued until nearly everyone on one side had been tagged.

Prisoner’s base was another game that was played many times. Like other games the rules were subject to change! Basically we played it like this: There were two teams – placed about 40 feet apart.. The members of each team lined up side by side at their base. Off to the side of each team was the “prison” – a square area large enough to hold several prisoners, if captured. The game began with each team allowing one of its members to be the prisoner of the opposite team. The objective of the game was to “free” the prisoner. In order to do that one had to reach the base where the prisoner was held – If in the process of trying to reach the prisoner the runner was tagged he/she also became a prisoner. The winning team was the team having the greatest number of prisoners at the end of the game. Again, rules were flexible and subject to change – especially since the rules were never written down and usually, if not always, recalled from memory.

Behind the school was a forested hill that we used to play on. Small saplings and brush could be pulled together, covered with burlap bags and then covered with dead leaves to provide “tent like” structures in which we sometimes ate our lunch. We could also travel through the woods to a cliff overlooking Sideling Hill Creek. I don’t recall that we actually went down the cliff to the creek, but I do remember eating the sweet bark from young black birch trees that grew on the cliff. Young black birch bark is very tender and has a strong winter green flavor.

There was a cleared path that ran directly up the hill a few feet from the back edge of the school house. When snow was on the ground we would sometimes sled ride down the path. We didn't go all the way to the top because it was very steep. Even going just part way up the hill gave us a very fast ride!

Indoor Games

Occasionally when the weather was too inclement we played a game indoors called Blind Man's Bluff. In preparation for the game the teacher's desk was moved out of the way and the recitation benches were move back toward the door. As much room as possible was made in the area where we wanted to play the game. One person was selected to be blindfolded. A towel or someone's scarf was tied around the person's head to insure that he/she could not see. The person whose eyes were covered was led to the center of the play space, turned around a couple times and then the game began. The other players went into the area where the blindfolded person was. In our school it was probably no more than ten or twelve persons playing at one time. The objective of the game was for the blindfolded person to catch or touch one of the other players and then guess the name of the person who had been touched. Sometimes when we played the game the person touched and identified would then be the blindfolded player, or sometimes, the touched and identified person left the game. The game continued until nearly everyone had been identified. Then, if time permitted, a new person was blindfolded and the game began all over again.

My Teachers

Grade 1

I remember well each of the teachers I had during my seven years at Barnes's Gap School. I was a young six year old when I started. My first teacher was a man named Gordon Winters. He taught one year only at my school; the other teachers I had taught two terms.

I still remember that first day – we had no orientation so I didn't know what to expect. I didn't know where the bathroom was – or, more accurately, the outdoor privy. Sometime during the afternoon of the first day I had a call from nature! I was a six year old who had to pee. Nothing unusual about that – little boys have to pee several times a day. Since moving from Pittsburgh we did not have indoor plumbing and had I been home I probably would not have walked all the way to the "outhouse" to take care of this small natural necessity. I probably would have gone behind a building or tree and "peed" So, what did I do on my first "need to go" at school? I went outside the schoolroom, walked down the porch steps and around the side of the building and – you guessed it, I peed! I went back into the schoolroom, sat down in my seat and awaited dismissal. I guess no one saw me. Nobody chided me for my unorthodox toilet behavior that day or the next! But after that first day I knew where the out door toilet was located.

Another memory I have of that first day was when the teacher asked me my name, I said, "Billy." My oldest sister piped up and said, "I think it's Billy William."

When I went home that afternoon I was very disgruntled – the teacher had not given me any books – I did not want to go back the second day! My mother, or someone, assured me I would get some books, soon. I did!

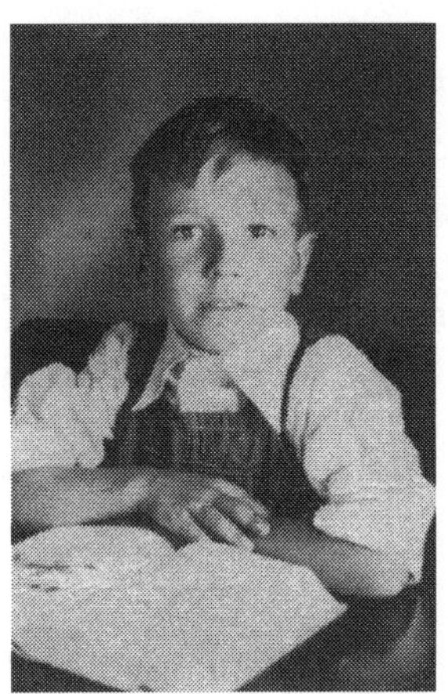

My first grade picture

Mr. Winters must have known how badly I wanted to learn to read. As soon as I finished one of the basic readers he found another for me. In fact, I remember well that one of the first grade readers I used had my mother's name in it. It had to have been purchased between 1910 and 1915 – my mother would have been a student in the primary grades at that time. I was using the same book in 1934. The book had a strong emphasis on phonics – pictures of animals with sounds that they made – or emphasis on the letter with which the animal's name started. My strongest academic competitor at Barnes's Gap School was a girl named Betty Smith. She continued to be my strongest academic challenger for the next seven years.

The distance of one mile was pretty far for six year old legs – especially when the roads were drifted with snow or covered with ice during the winter months and in the spring the dirt roads were very muddy and deeply rutted by automobile traffic. I had a "savior" though. My neighbor, Julian Shanholtz, was about fifteen years old, and he helped me get through some of those drifts and lifted me across some of the deepest ruts and mud puddles that had to be crossed. My mother was so grateful to Julian that at the end of the year she bought him some small gift; I remember giving it to him. I'm certain he was surprised because his helpfulness to me was never done with the expectation of a gift.

Grade 2

My second grade teacher was a young woman by the name of Miss Shank. I don't remember very much about my academic life that year, except that I enjoyed reading. I do, however, remember a couple incidents that had a rather strong impact on me – I still remember them! My neighbor, Robert Shanholtz, a few months younger than I, was in the first grade. I knew his name was Robert, I played with him at home, I always called him Robert. On this particular day I decided to call him Bob or Bobby! He protested to me – reminding me that his name was Robert. But, I didn't stop. Finally, he told Miss Shank what I was doing. She called me up to her desk and confronted me with my infraction. I admitted to it – and she told me in no uncertain terms not to do it anymore! I said I wouldn't – but I tried to mount a defense. It was a very feeble one, I said, "But he calls me Billy, and my name is William." She did not buy it! Never again, though, did I call my friend Bob or Bobby!

Miss Shank, top row extreme right, my second grade teacher.
I am standing in the first row, extreme left

Then there was the incident that occurred on the last day of school! The last day is a great day for kids regardless of what grade. On this particular last day Miss Shank had brought a young friend of hers to school, named Freddie – he was about my age. A group of us were eating lunch along side of the school building when for some reason that I have long since forgotten, Freddie and I got into a scuffle! Within a few seconds we were flailing away at each other. I apparently landed one of my wild punches on his lip. It began to bleed and the scuffle ended as quickly as it had begun. Freddie went into the school house and the teacher asked Freddie about his bleeding lip. He told her. Next, I was called in and my teacher told me that my punishment for fighting would be to remain in my seat the rest of the afternoon. I learned a lesson that day: Don't get into a fight on the last day of school with a kid named Freddie – who's a friend of the teacher!

Grades 3 and 4

I had the same teacher for grades 3 and 4. His name was Mr. Lewis Deneen. I remember him very well. He always played games with us out on the playground. To an eight or nine year old he was about the fastest runner I had ever seen. When we played tag – it seemed he could always catch me in about a half dozen steps. When we played ball he could hit a home run every time he came up to bat! I liked him in the classroom, too. He allowed me to read as much as I wanted. Many years later he told me my favorite reading material was Winnie the Pooh! I remember other material that I enjoyed reading, too – especially during the fourth grade. I don't remember the name of the history book that we used, but I do remember that I enjoyed taking it home and reading it before going to bed. I would get very sleepy – but I didn't want to stop reading so I washed my face with cold water in order to stay awake and read a little longer.

Mr. Lewis Deneen, extreme right, grade 4.
I am the fourth student from the left in the front row

I still remember a class incident that occurred in Mr. Deneen's class. One of the girls was supposed to read a story about Captain John Smith. Part of the story related to an episode in John Smith's life prior to his coming to this country. Captain Smith was fighting the Turks. According to the story John Smith slew three Turks! Well, to the little farm girl who was relating the story, "Turks" referred to turkeys that they had on their farm. So when she got to the part of the story where John Smith had combat with the Turks, she said, "And when John Smith sneaked upon the Turks they saw him – and flew away! Obviously, the little farm girl's frame of reference was her experience on the farm – the idea that "Turks" was the name of soldiers from Turkey was completely outside of her conceptual framework.

Grade 5

Miss Shank was assigned to Barnes's Gap again – three years previously she had been my second grade teacher. She already knew the students at the school although during the academic year a new family moved into the area and three new students were added – three girls. I enjoyed fifth grade very much. Each month we would receive an orange crate full of books – apparently the books were circulated throughout the rural schools in the county. Those of us who enjoyed reading looked forward to the arrival of a different set of books from which to select new and different reading material.

In a one room school instruction given to one class can be heard by everyone else in the school room. I enjoyed listening to the class discussions held with the sixth, seventh, and eighth graders. Every student in the school had an opportunity to have a preview of what learning would be introduced the next year! To me this has always seemed to be a great plus for students attending a one room school. Miss Shank was especially good to me, in fact she double promoted Betty Smith and me to grade seven!

Christmas in our very rural school was always memorable. But the one Christmas event that stands out above all others occurred during the fifth grade when Miss Shank was the teacher. Let me share it with you:

A Christmas Surprise

I had risen early that morning. It was the last day of school before the Christmas vacation. The night before I had laid out my knickers suit – I was going to be dressed up today! I hated those knickers – I was ten years old and wanted long pants. But, my mother evidently liked knickers, because that's all I had to wear if I wanted to get "dressed up". Anyway, it would be a special day – a few weeks earlier we had all "exchanged names". Each person in that small, one room school had written his/her name on a slip of paper and dropped it into a hat. The hat was then passed up and down the isles, and every student reached into the hat and drew a slip of paper. The hat was held high enough so that no one could see the name of the person whose name was drawn. A

Christmas gift would be bought for the person whose name was on the slip of paper.

The gifts purchased probably cost no more than a quarter – that would have been the high end! For the last week or so before our vacation would begin many students had placed their gifts under the tree. The tree was a rather scraggly white pine that the "big boys," a couple of 8th graders, had cut in the woods behind the schoolhouse. It had been decorated with paper "chains" made from green and red construction paper, odds and ends of cast off glass balls that the children had brought to school, and the branches were nearly covered with icicles and red and green tinsel provided by the teacher. The interior walls of the classroom were covered with children's Christmas artwork that had been accumulating for the past three weeks. Oh yes, there were several Santa's on the wall whose arms and legs were attached with knotted string in such a way that when a string attached to the back was pulled, Santa became animated – kicking his arms and legs in opposite directions.

Many gifts bought by students were already placed under the tree. I discovered that the person who had drawn my name was my academic competitor, Betty Smith. She and I were the only two students in fifth grade. I saw my name on a neatly wrapped gift in bright, red paper. The shape of the package indicated that it must be a tie! Of, course, I would much rather have seen a package that resembled a pocket knife with my name on it!

The morning session proceeded as usual. After the noon lunch and play period ended we sang a few Christmas songs – the finale of the afternoon would be when the gifts from under the tree were distributed and the teacher would give us our "Christmas Treat" – typically, that consisted of a small commercially made box filled with candies selected by the teacher, and an orange. – then, we'd all walk to our homes. However, today the familiar routine changed. During the singing of Jingle Bells – all the students heard a noise behind them. Heads and bodies turned in the direction of the sound! On that wall of the classroom was a ladder leading to the floor above the ceiling.

This upper room was empty – but could have served the purpose of permitting someone to check the safety of the stovepipe that went up through the classroom ceiling and entered a chimney that was supported by joists in the ceiling. The schoolroom was heated by a large cast iron wood burning stove located in the center of the room. A trapdoor closed the ceiling opening at the top of the ladder – and, I suspect most of the students didn't even know it was there. Every student upon hearing the sound – all twenty of us, focused on the upper rungs of the ladder – Imagine the sounds of those preadolescents when they saw a pair of black boots drop from the now opened trapdoor and start down the ladder. It was Santa Claus – complete with red suit and a pack over his shoulder! He descended the ladder and walked to the front of the room, greeted us, and then reached into his pack and began pulling out boxes of candy; giving one to each of us! Then he began picking up gifts from under the tree and calling the name of the person to receive the gift. Eventually, the name of every student was called and each student received his gift from Santa's hands. There was a polite "Thank you" from everyone! Yes, I got that tie from Betty, a pretty red one! When the last gift was handed out Santa wished all of us a Merry Christmas and walked back the isle, opened the door, and left the building. After a few remarks from our teacher, Miss Shank, we were dismissed and our Christmas vacation had begun.

Immediately the "big boys," followed by practically every other boy in the school, started the search for Santa – the search didn't last long! Behind the schoolhouse was a steep wooded hill. Santa was found sitting at the base of a large oak tree near the top of the hill with his Santa costume on the ground beside him. Little Billy, about five years old, was a visitor and guest that day of Miss Shank. He followed the rest of the boys in their search for Santa—Finally, Billy caught up with everyone else and stood looking at Santa "out of uniform". With a look of disappointment on his face and a bit of disgust and doubt in his voice, he pointed a finger at Santa and proclaimed, "You're not Santa, you're Buck!" Santa, or Buck, it seems was a good friend of the teacher, as well as Billy! I don't know if Billy ever regained his faith in a real Santa Claus – but I do know that for the twenty pupils who witnessed Santa descending that ladder it was an event and a day that was never to be forgotten.

Miss Shank was a special teacher to me. Like so many teachers of that era who taught in one room schools – she did so with minimal supplies, support, textbooks, and other materials that today's teacher need and demand. Additionally, she served as the custodian, school nurse, coach, counselor, and performed whatever tasks that needed to be done, all this, in addition to teaching the 3 R's to eight grades of children ranging in age from six to sixteen.. And, for a salary that was far, far below today's minimum wage! Miss Shank, probably no more than 21 years old, did the above with the efficiency of a teacher with many more years of experience.

Nearly fifty years after the Santa incident that is related above, I visited my fifth grade teacher. I told her how my younger sister and I still remembered "Santa" coming down the ladder and passing out Christmas gifts. She remembered, too. Her comment was one of praise for "Buck" – "That was really nice of him, wasn't it, to sit up there all morning and come down the ladder in the afternoon to surprise all you kids." I agreed – but, it was really "Miss Shank" who deserved a great deal of thanks and credit for providing a classroom of students with a Christmas memory that would last a life time.

Another incident that occurred during my fifth year relates to an accident I had in school. I call it, "Training for a track meet."

Training for a Track Meet

It was early spring and maybe the teacher, Miss Shank, mentioned it, or perhaps one of my schoolmates remarked that in a few weeks there would be a track meet at Warfordsburg High School. Actually, it was a county meet and the four high schools in the county would compete in various track and field events. Elementary schools were invited, too, but our little school, Barnes's Gap, never competed. Some of us boys thought we would like to participate. The high jump appealed to me – I didn't know much about techniques, but I had been to a track meet at the high school as an observer a year ago – and since then I had practice jumping over fences and gates. I considered running in one of the dashes – when I'd mention running to my dad he would say to me, "You should be able to run fast; you have nothing to carry but your shoes"! He was making a reference to my skinny body and pipe stem legs.

One of the first jobs we boys had to do in preparation for the meet was dig a landing pit for our high jump practice. The next day one of the boys brought a mattock and shovel and after checking out a few possible sites we decided on a location at the far side of the playground. It was a sodded area and the site was in a slight depression. When it was time for the first recess we were ready to start making the excavation. It was in the early spring and we found the ground soft and the digging easy. By the end of the day – after working during the lunch period and afternoon recess our pit was finished. We had two more tasks to do before the practice could begin. One, we had to get two uprights and drive nails into them at the right positions and then get a crossbar that we could place over the nails that we'd driven into the uprights. The second task was to get several sacks full of wood shavings and fill the pit. Securing the up rights and the shavings would be no problem – about three quarters of a mile from the school there was a lumber planning mill which was owned by Charles Hixon, his son, Junior, was a student at school – and so was his grandson, Billy Perkins. We could go into the woods behind the school and cut a sapling and use it for the crossbar. The following day we filled the pit with shavings and planted the uprights on the front edge on either side of the pit. After cutting our crossbar – which was about ten feet long and ranged in diameter from about 2 inches at the butt to about one inch at the small end. The height of the bar could be adjusted from a foot and a half above the ground to four feet above. When the bar was at it highest point it wasn't at all difficult for me to walk under it!

Well, with the completion of the pit – practice began in earnest the next day. After lunch I was one of the first to make a jump. No problem – the height was 18 inches! All the boys made that jump. Actually, some of the bigger boys ran straight at it as though it were a hurdle and practically stepped over it. But I didn't. I used a scissors technique. Soon the bar – I should say pole, was up to thirty inches. Heck, I thought, that's not as high as the fences and gates I've been jumping. I was fully confident that I would clear the bar with much space to spare. I made my approach – running on a slight angle to the bar and lifted my right leg and then the left, – my technique wasn't very polished! Somehow or other gravity conspired against me. I barely got the right leg over the bar and my left leg and arm didn't clear it at all. Instead my arm got caught on the underside of the bar dragging it into the pit and I landed on top of the bar! My arm, just above the wrist, was under the bar. It wasn't until I got up and looked at the arm and saw the "bend" in it that I realized I had injured it. At the moment it really did not hurt that much. One of the "big" boys, James Shanholtz, realized that I had probably broken my arm. He walked with me back to the school – a couple hundred yards from the jump pit—and told the teacher what had happened.

There was no telephone at the school and the teacher did not have a car. She asked James if he would walk with me to my home – which was a mile from the school. James was a good choice because his home was only about a tenth of a mile from our house and he was very mature boy. We started for my home – actually the arm was not yet that painful. After about twenty minutes we reached my home. But, there was nobody there! My parents were at my grandparents' home—a mile from where I lived! So, we started down the dirt road to my grandparents. When we arrived James explained what had happened to my arm. By now it was somewhat swollen – not a great deal but enough that it was noticeable, plus it was starting to hurt, especially when I tried to move my wrist. It took a few minutes to find my dad – and my Uncle Ted, who lived on the farm with my grandparents. As soon as possible we were on our way to a doctor in Hancock, Maryland – about 30 to 45 minutes away. James, in the meantime walked home.

My uncle parked his 1934 Plymouth in front of the doctor's office. We walked in and there was no waiting! The doctor looked at the arm, pressed on the place where it had a distinct bow – made a comment about the arm being swollen and took me back into a little room away from the waiting room. I remember his telling my uncle to take hold of my upper forearm. The doctor took a good grip of my hand and the two started pulling in opposite directions. That hurt! No anesthesia, no x-ray – the doctor and my uncle pulled my arm until the distortion was no longer to be seen. Then he put a metal plate under the forearm and mixed a powder and water together, dipped some gauze strips in it and started wrapping the metal plate and the arm. Soon I had a forearm about the size of my thigh! He fashioned a sling from some white cloth, placed it under the arm and tied the ends together behind my neck to support the arm; then my dad and uncle took me home.

Oh, yes, I remember the doctor said to me, "You're a tough boy, you didn't cry a bit"! No, I didn't, but I certainly felt like it when he and my uncle had what appeared to me to be a "tug of war" with my hand and forearm. I had the cast on my arm for about six weeks; it was no longer white, by now it was pretty dirty. My dad took me in to see the doctor one day and the cast was removed. The arm looked as good as new and actually felt fine – but, I faked pain every once in awhile when

I thought it was to my advantage – for example, if there was a bucket of water to be carried or a chore that I didn't like to do, the pain would become quite severe! By mid to late summer the arm was completely healed. I went right back to jumping fences and gates – but never again did I jump over a makeshift bar to land in a pit of shavings!

Grades 7 and 8

Mrs. Ada McKee was my teacher during the last two years at Barnes's Gap. For me they were excellent years. She was one of the best teachers I ever had. Mrs. McKee, a couple years older than my mother, had attended Barnes Gap along with my mother and other members of mother's family. As was true at that time of all the teachers I had at Barnes's Gap – none had a college degree. In later years some would earn a BS degree. In their early years of teaching, however, they needed state certification only. To their great credit what they may have lacked in formal course work they more than made up for in their conscientiousness, concern for student, and desire to be the best teacher they could be.

Students attending Barnes Gap School in 1940.
I am the second student in the third row

Before entering high school students had to pass an entrance examination. Mrs. McKee certainly prepared her students well. I remember when I was taking the eighth grade examination that I felt very prepared in every area of the examination. In retrospect it seems to me that I must have read a different book every week. On Friday afternoons she allowed me to tell the rest of the school about a book I was reading. It was she who brought her own copy of Erich Remarque's, *All Quiet on the Western Front*, for me to read. After I read it, I recall her saying to me, "There was some down to earth language in the book, wasn't there?" Then, there was Jack London – I journeyed with him in *Call of the Wild* and *White Fang* – in my mind my mongrel dog morphed into whatever adventure the dog hero in Jack London's stories was engaged. It's true, I didn't know much about Jack London, the author, when I was a twelve year old, but the interest that Mrs. McKee generated in me for his books motivated me years later to learn more about the author and his era. There was another book that as a twelve year old I loved – It was Edward Eggleston's *The Hoosier School Master*. Many years later as an adult, I re-read the book. Oh, I read every page – but, I'll have to admit, it was not the exciting book that I remembered reading as a child!

She believed, also, in having her eighth graders memorize and recite poems. – I can still recite verses from two of Helen Hunt Jackson's poems, "September" and "October's Bright Blue Weather"; it took me a little longer to learn and recite John Greenleaf Whittier's "Barefoot Boy", and "In School Days", but I still enjoy those poems. Simple, they were, maybe overly sentimental, – but had I not learned them well enough to recite them as a twelve year old, I wonder if I would enjoy them as much as I do today? Yes, we learned several of Henry Wadsworth Longfellow's poems – the two that come to mind now are, "O Ship of State" and "Under the Spreading Chestnut Tree". Probably one of my favorites poems was John Masefield's, "Sea Fever" – I must go down to the seas again … I thoroughly enjoyed learning that one – when I first read that poem I had never been close to the sea! Many questions in the eighth grade examination were based on the books and poems that Mrs. McKee encouraged me to read.

Not only do I have pleasant memories of what happened inside the classroom, but also of events associated with the playground. Let me share a memory with you.

The Bicycle

It was the last day of school, always a special day for any school age child. This last day, however, was a special one for me. I was in the eighth grade, one of no more than about 20 students in the entire school. Mrs. Ada McKee was my teacher. During the morning hours of the last day the teacher used the time to collect all the books from each of the eight grades and to take care of routine tasks that needed to be completed before the term ended. Then, after we ate lunch, the entire afternoon was "play time". One of my best friends, Billy Perkins, rode his bicycle to school that day. I didn't have a bike, but I certainly wanted one. I recall Mrs. McKee saying to me out on the playground, "Billy, can you ride a bike?" Frankly I wasn't sure if I could or not. Well, Billy told me I could ride his bike as much as I wanted to that afternoon. And I did! It was a pretty dilapidated old bicycle – dented, wired on fenders, scratched paint, smooth tires, and, when braking, I remember you had to pedal backwards two or three revolutions before braking was effected. Billy, a natural born salesman, noted how much I like that bike told me he wanted to sell it. My immediate question was: How much? He said he wanted nine dollars for it! I didn't have that much money but the amount did give me some hope – I thought, just maybe, I could get the money from my parents. I told Billy that perhaps I'd buy it – if I did I'd go to his house tomorrow morning to get it. He lived about two miles from where I lived and for a 12 year old that wasn't a very great distance to walk, especially if I'd be riding home on my very own bicycle.

All afternoon and early evening I thought about owning that bicycle. In my mind's eye I could see those old dented, wired on fenders replaced with new ones that I would order from the Montgomery Ward catalog – I'd paint them a royal blue color and then put a white trim on the fenders like I had seen on the new bikes in a bicycle shop in a nearby town. Yes, I would take the hub apart and buy a set of disc for it and repair the braking problem. Indeed, that old bike would soon look and run like a new one. But, first of all, I had to own it!

We lived on a small farm and money was never in abundance. Sometimes, during the spring and summer, my dad would work a few days doing road maintenance and the money earned would help to buy the necessities needed by a family of four children and two adults. The work was seasonal and couldn't be depended on – I knew that getting nine dollars from my dad would not be easy. I remember spending a considerable amount of time thinking about a strategy I could use that would be most effective. Yes, I would promise to pay it back, I'd do extra work, maybe even promise not to tease my sisters so much – but, I finally decided I'd use just a straight-forward approach – I would tell him about the bicycle and let him know how much I wanted it – and hope he would come through!

That evening about 6 o'clock when he came home I met him at the gate. I told him about the bicycle and that my friend, Billy, had allowed me to ride it most of the afternoon and that I really wanted it! Besides, I said, "Billy only wants nine dollars for it."

He looked at me and simply said, "I don't have nine dollars that I can give you." Of course, I was expecting an answer like that – and even as a 12 year old I knew it was true. But still, the desire for that bike was a lot stronger than my acceptance of the economics that prompted my dad's response. Before going to bed that night I made a couple more attempts at persuading him to change his mind – even in front of my mother. The answer was always the same, "I don't have nine dollars that I can give you." No anger or hint of disgust in his voice, just a matter of fact statement.

I got up early the next morning when dad did. At the breakfast table, in what I knew would be my last attempt, I again made my plea for the nine dollars. This time there was no answer – he just continued eating his breakfast. I finished eating my breakfast, got up and walked to the door realizing that I wouldn't be riding my own bicycle this day! In a moment or so he got up from the table, walked over to the kitchen stove, picked up his lunch box that was on the edge of it, and walked toward the door where I was standing. When he was along side of where I stood, he reached out with his left hand and nudged my right hand – in his palm he had a small roll of bills that he placed in my hand. He didn't say a word – just kept on walking across the porch, down the steps, through the gate and down the road to where he would be working that day. I quickly counted those bills – there were nine! Within minutes I was walking – running down the dusty, dirt road that led to my friend's house. The transaction with Billy was a quick one. I was soon home with my bike!

That evening my dad sat on the front porch watching me ride my bicycle up and down the road in front of our house. He didn't say anything—he just smiled. During that summer I hoed a lot of corn for my grandfather at ten cents a row, and spent every penny fixing up that bike – yes, new fenders, tires, a luggage carrier, saddle bags, hand grips, paint, and I soon learned how to take that New Departure rear hub apart and replace the parts needed to ensure that the brakes worked. It did look and ride like a new bike!

As a boy that was the only bicycle I ever owned. I kept it for four years and near the end of my senior year in high school I asked dad if he'd take me to a nearby town where I was going to try to sell it to a hardware dealer who bought used bikes. He said he would and I loaded the bike into the trunk of our car. The store owner offered me twelve dollars. I accepted. I guess we were both satisfied with the deal.

My dad has been gone for many, many years. In fact, I'm now within a few years of his age when he passed away. And, I'm haunted by the simple fact that I don't believe I ever thanked him for the sacrifice he made just to make a twelve year old boy happy! The nine dollars given to me that morning was probably all the money he had. But, I'd like to believe that the smile he had on his face as he sat on the front porch watching me ride my bike up and down the road the first evening I owned it – indicated that he understood the gratitude I felt. I've learned, too, as a father and grandfather, that when you do things for people you love, you don't do them just to receive a vocal, "thank you". Anyway, Dad, here's a belated, very sincere, "Thank you, for buying me that bicycle."

Barnes's Gap School Closes

Barnes's Gap School was closed sometime in the 1950's For a short time the students who would have attended that one room school were transported to another one room school, Center School, about five miles away. Eventually, all one room schools were closed in the township and elementary students were transported to the old high school at Warfordsburg that continued to have an elementary program. Today all student are transported to a new, very modern elementary school in the Southern Fulton County School District.

Warfordsburg High School as it appears today

Warfordsburg High School

After passing the examination at the close of eighth grade – the one required for entrance to high school – I entered high school the following September. The school is shown above. By standards of today it was not a large school. At the time it seemed very large to me. After all, I had spent the previous seven years in a one room school! The enrollment was probably not over two hundred and the total number of faculty was probably only seven or eight. The building principal, Mr. Gordon Charlton, also taught all science courses – biology, chemistry and physics. He was one of my favorite persons at the school; I respected him as a principal, I thought he was a great science teacher, and, for me at least, he served as a guidance counselor. He often spoke to me about going to college. One Saturday night in the town of Hancock, Maryland I happened to see him and his wife. I was still in the navy and he spoke to me about what I planned to do after I was discharged from the service. He encouraged me to think about becoming a biology teacher. Teaching was certainly a profession that I least wanted to pursue while a high school student! Apparently he was persuasive – I cancelled my acceptance at two universities – with majors in forestry and agriculture, to enter a teacher training institution. What was my initial major? Biology! The persuasive power of a good teacher!!!

I enjoyed my four years at Warfordsburg High School. Compared to facilities available in most high schools today our high school had many deficiencies. We had a very poor library, the selection of courses was very limited, and the facilities for science teaching were practically non-existent. A few chemicals were kept in an unlocked cabinet in one of the classrooms. I say unlocked because I remember very well when a good friend, Marvin Oakman, and I opened the door and found a jar containing a piece of sodium immersed in kerosene. We cut off a piece and took it to the lavatory that was next door. There we filled the lavatory bowl with water and dropped small pieces of the sodium into it. We watched it sputter and melt and, I believe the gas produced burst into a flame. Obviously, we really didn't know what we were doing, but I must confess both of us were pretty fascinated with what we saw! Fortunately, the science teacher did not catch us – he was also the school principal. Despite the limitations of the facility, the high school teachers were conscientious individuals doing the best job they could under the circumstances in which they had to teach.

The high school curriculum, for the most part, was not a college preparatory one. Actually, during the time period that I attended the high school most of my classmates were enrolled in the Vocational Agriculture program. Apparently my interests were a little different – I recall taking Latin and French instead!

Our sports teams were unremarkable, at least those on which I played. I was a terrible basketball player; perhaps a little bit better in baseball. To my knowledge – at least during my tenure there – – there was nothing like a championship team – in anything! But, I remember some pretty good athletes whose high school sports activities were cut short when they were drafted or volunteered for service in World War II.

There were only a couple students from my class that went on to higher education. The small number going to college was not because of intellectual or academic deficiencies, but rather because of economics or simply because there was so little encouragement to do so by parents. The school drew its population from a very rural area where small-scale farming was the primary vocation. There were not many role models from occupations or professions that required a college education to inspire young people. Also, there were no guidance counselors to advise students with an academic bent that there were professions they might want to consider that required a college education.

I do not recall there being any major problems in discipline among the high school student body. Yes, I remember the principal having to "take hold" of a student on one or two occasions and helping him to his seat! But the infraction that brought on that type discipline was probably related to being out of an assigned seat, talking too loudly, or unruly student behavior. A student caught smoking a cigarette in the boiler room could very well be subject to some mild punishment if caught! The most serious infraction that I ever had to answer for was chewing gum in class. I recall one such incident very well. It was during a study period and just before going into the room I had put my last stick of "Juicy Fruit" gum in my mouth. The teacher monitoring the room was one that I knew very well. She taught Latin and French and she knew me, too. I believe I was the only male from my class that was taking those languages. The study period had only been in session for a few minutes and apparently I was too engrossed in whatever I was doing to notice that I was chewing rather vigorously on my Juicy Fruit! I don't know why but I happened to look up at the desk where the teacher was sitting. Her eyes were fixed on me – she didn't say a word;

but she did point to the waste paper can in the corner. I understood the signal perfectly – I put my gum into a small piece of tablet paper, folded it, and walked up to the waste paper can where I tossed it. I was aware that the teacher was watching me every step of the way! Nothing was said and I went back to my seat and resumed my work.

I suspect many teachers today would be grateful if the worst discipline problem they faced was an adolescent chewing gum!!! In retrospect, I believe all my classmates, yes, the entire school body, by standards of today, would be considered a very, very docile group of students!

One of the most constructive memories that I have related to Warfordsburg High School occurred during my senior year. An assignment had been made to read a certain journal article that dealt with foreign affairs. The teacher had a very informal manner of teaching, which for me, at least, made his assignments easy to ignore or not complete in a timely manner. During this class period he walked back to the seat where I was sitting. He said to me, "Bill, what did you think of the article you read?" "I didn't read it," I said. An obvious response from him was, "Why not?" It was then that I responded in a way that was deserving of the "slap down" I got. I was so bold as to say, "What that author has to say is only his opinion!" "Well, Bill", he said, "that author is a lot more qualified to express his opinion than you are to criticize it!" I remember nothing else from that course; I do remember that well deserved "put down."

The school has not been used as a high school for many years. Today the windows are covered with plywood the doors are locked – apparently the school district has not yet found a new use for this old building that served many students so well for many, many years.

Chapter 6

Grandfather Northcraft's Farm

Description

My grandfather owned a large farm. His father had purchased the original acreage sometime during the 1860's. The Northcraft family was an early settler in Southampton Township, in adjoining Bedford County. The name first appears in the 1798 Census. My grandfather's name appears in the 1870 census as a three year old! The land purchased by my great grandfather was part of land located in a gap in Rays Hill/Town Hill Mountain. The gap took its name from the first settler. It was known as Barnes's Gap. According to an account found in the *History of Bedford, Somerset and Fulton Counties*, Barnes located in an old Indian Camp and made a clearing, but was primarily a hunter. Other than the reference made in the work just cited I know of no documentation that corroborates that the site was an old Indian camp. However, Indian arrow heads were found in abundance and, perhap still are in certain fields on the farm. Especially in a field directly below where the present farm house is located. As a boy I used to search for and find beautiful arrow heads and pieces of flint and other materials used in the making of arrow heads, spear points, and stone implements used by Indians – the items found and the stone chips were unlike other rocks and minerals found in that particular area. A spring nearby flows from the base of a hill. The location would have been an excellent site for an Indian encampment. So strong was the spring flow that regardless of how dry the summer, enough water poured forth that a stream flowed down through an adjoining field. When corn was planted in that field my grandfather would sometimes divert some of the flow into rows of corn – one could readily see the difference in the green coloring of the corn between that which was irrigated and that which was not! In the first years of farming my grandfather was aided very much by his unmarried brother, George. Over the years they added many acres to the original farm. Much of the land lay on either side of Sideling Hill creek – deep, rich, fertile soil. Some of the land added later included ridge and steep valley lands characteristic of the ridge and valley terrain of Union Township..

View of my grandfather's house and farm buildings from the face of the mountain directly behind the buildings. The picture was taken about 1960.

My grandfather married and started his own family about 1900. His wife, was also a descendant of a pioneer family of Bedford County. Eventually, there would be three daughters followed by three sons. His unmarried brother, George, remained at home and continued to be very much a part of the farm operation. Hard work, plus business acumen, served the Northcraft Brothers well. My grandfather established a general store, and a post office, with the family name was located there in 1905 – both of which served the community for many years. His general store served people living within a rather large radius of the store. I heard many interesting stories related to his store and the people who patronized it.. I recall one that my uncle related to me involving my mother. Apparently, her father had sold one of his patrons a small milk pitcher. The day after the purchase the man brought it back to the store and said to my grandfather, "That pitcher you sold me yesterday had a cracked lip – my daughter almost cut her lip on it last night." My mother, who was only about ten years old, heard the customer's comment. Not being the most diplomatic little girl, but one who knew what pitchers were for, spontaneously said, "Well, she shouldn't be drinking out of the pitcher!" Her father and mother were not a bit amused by the comment! Her father not wanting to lose a customer – was a firm believer in "The Customer Is Always Right!" His immediate reaction was to apologize and give the customer another pitcher. Unfortunately for my mother, she was living in an era and an area where it was generally accepted that "children were to be seen and not heard." She was scolded by both mother and father! My mother use to laugh about the customer who repeatedly came to the store and asked for "white shoe blackening". I guess he meant white shoe polish!!! I remember the store and some of the customers who continued to patronize it well into the 1940's I especially remember the hand operated gasoline pumps that stood in front of the store. I played with them many times! Also, I recall my grandfather filling the kerosene cans for his customers from the manually operated pump on the kerosene tank kept inside the store. During that time period many of the people that patronized his store used kerosene as fuel for their oil burning lamps

.Each day about noon time a postal employee from a larger post office would arrive with mail that would be distributed from my grandfather's post office. Grandfather or my grandmother, would sort the mail and place it in the little cubicles to be picked up later by patrons. Typically, there would be several people in the store sitting around a wood burning stove in the winter time, talking with each other or sharing in the gossip of the day. Eventually fewer and fewer people got their mail at the Northcraft Post Office. The post office was discontinued in 1941.

During the early 1900's in addition to operating the general store, my grandfather hauled farm produce to Cumberland, Maryland in a wagon drawn by two or four horses – no small feat considering the distance and the terrain traveled. It took two days to get to Cumberland. On the route there was a stopping place where grandfather would stay the night. My mother who apparently went with him on occasions told me that he had a canvas over the wagon and a lighted lantern provided some heat for the occupants during cold weather trips.

During these years additional land was added to the growing size of the farm. Additionally, he bought mountain land that would later be sold for purposes other than farming.

My grandfather's farm became a part of my life shortly after we moved from Pittsburgh, Pennsylvania. Not too long after our move my great Uncle George sent me to the barn for an "open ring" – he was making some repair on a harness. I brought back to him something completely unrelated to an "open ring" – I had absolutely no idea what an open ring was!!! Not very understanding was he of my lack of knowledge – he said to one of my uncles nearby, "They didn't get that boy out of the city soon enough!"

Working on the Farm

When I was about seven years old I started hoeing corn with "grandpap" and George. No matter how fast I tried to hoe, I could never pass my grandfather! I could get by George, but "grandpap" was always a few paces ahead – after awhile I gave up trying—I was always hoping he'd say, "Time for a drink and a rest"!

After a few years, in addition to hoeing corn, I was sent to the field with a triple shovel plow and a horse and instead of chopping out the weeds with a hoe, I plowed them out or covered them with dirt from the three shovel plow! That job really wasn't too bad if the ground was smooth and not too many stones – the plow would glide along very smoothly between the rows of corn dislodging or covering the weeds that came up between the rows or between the stocks of corn. If the ground were rocky – the job was a bit more difficult. One of the shovels might be bumped into the corn row and take out a few stocks before I could get the plow back to the center of the row.

I did enjoy riding the horse to the field – especially if I had recently seen a cowboy movie. My uncles and grandfather didn't appreciate my making that old plow horse run at a gallop to the fields! "You'll make him stiff," they would say. Maybe they were right, I didn't know about that – I was certain it was fun to mimic that cowboy star that I had seen in a movie!.

I haven't forgotten the embarrassment I felt the day I had trouble getting the harness on the horse – I had taken it off the peg where it was kept inside the horse stable. Apparently, I didn't have quite enough strength to lift it up over the horse's back and places the hames over the collar. Somehow or other I got it turned around and the crupper was facing the front of the horse! That's when one of my uncles came into the stable. The crupper is that part of a harness that goes under the horse's tail to prevent the harness from sliding forward. Well, you can imagine the comment! "Don't you know the difference between the horses head and his rear end?" I had to live with that for a long time.

Some of the farm work that I remember most vividly was related to making hay. Before the tractor became widely used on grandfather's farm, horses were primarily used. Two horses were used to pull the mowing machine. I was never entrusted with that chore. There was no mistaking the clicking sound of the sickle bar extending about six feet from the side of the mower – as the bar moved through the standing clover, timothy, alfalfa, or whatever the crop might be, one could see the swath of freshly cut hay falling backward over the sickle bar. Cut hay has to be allowed to dry before it can be processed any further. "Make hay while the sun shines" – while one may give a broader interpretation to that old proverb, its literal translation speaks to making hay! During the early to mid 1930's to the very early 1940's making hay was a very labor intensive farm job. After cutting and allowing it to dry for a period of time (depending on the humidity in the air), I was sometimes asked to use an old "dump" rake pulled by two horses. The operator sat on a seat just in front of the teeth and controlled the action of the teeth by depressing a foot treadle. When a sufficient amount of hay was held by the teeth, the treadle was depressed and the bar holding the teeth would rise, thus dropping the hay. As one went across the field the hay was dropped in such a fashion as to produce a row. If sufficiently dry the farm hands would follow the row and stack the hay in small "doodles" approximately four feet in diameter. Forking the hay into the doodles was something a boy my age could do – I did this many times. When the hay was deemed to be dry enough the hay wagon was driven along the row of "doodles" and, in my experience, my two six foot tall uncles with long handled pitch forks started forking the hay onto the wagon. I wasn't tall enough for that job! It was always my job to be the "loader" which meant that I had to position the hay forked onto the wagon in such a way that the load was evenly distributed. My goal was to have nice square corners as high as the hay could be piled onto the wagon – then, taper it slightly higher toward the middle of the load. One of my uncles would pull the "boom pole" from underneath the running gears of the wagon and push it to the top of the load. I would then slide the one end of it into the inverted metal V at the front of the wagon. The middle of a strong rope was secured around the other end of the boom pole. Both my uncles would pull down on each side of the rope secured to the boom pole and then tie the ends to opposite sides of the wagon frame. This helped prevent the load from shifting or, even falling off the wagon on the way back to the barn.

When the wagon load of hay reached the barn the horses pulled the wagon onto the barn floor between the two mows. My grandfather's barn was large – there were two mows on either side of the barn floor. Sometimes the mow on the right side would be filled with grain, usually wheat. It would remain there until thrashed sometime during the latter part of summer. The mow on the left was usually reserved for hay. Pushing the hay around in the mow in order that it would be stacked evenly as the hay was brought in from the barn was often part of my job. Hay was removed from the wagon by means of a "hay fork" – a two pronged device that was pushed into the loose hay on the wagon. The fork was attached to heavy rope that was drawn over a couple of pulley attached to timbers above the mow. Of course, the other end of the rope was attached to a singletree pulled by one horse for a distance that was sufficient to draw the hay to a position where it would be dropped in the mow. There was a trip rope that the person operating the hay fork would pull when the bunch of hay was drawn over the spot where it was to be dropped.

The hay mow was not a pleasant place to work! The dust was terrible – worse with certain kinds of hay. And, the heat! The higher the hay was piled in the mow, the closer the person in the mow was to the tin roof and the hotter the temperature! When I worked in the hay mow it was usually without a shirt – after a half hour or so in that environment I'd come out looking as though I had been dipped in some kind of oil and then sprinkled with black dust! Not a very pretty sight! The spring house was only a short distance from the barn – that was the first place I headed after coming out of the barn! I'm certain I drank more liquid than I lost in the hay mow.

Another interesting event on the farm for a young boy was threshing time. On my grandfather's farm the main road ran between the house and the barn. That road ran past the entrance to the barn floor – not more than fifty feet away.

Often when the grain to be threshed had been stored in one of the barn mows, the threshing machine was pushed onto the barn floor along side the mow in which the grain had been stored. The tractor providing power for the threshing machine had to be parked across the main road – which meant that the large belt that would go round the drive pulley on the tractor blocked the road when it was stretched across the road to go round the pulley on the threshing machine in the barn! Vehicles using the road would have to slow down and drive behind the tractor – the road was a little wider at this spot so no serious problems arose when road traffic had to pass behind the tractor.

I remember there were two persons that provided threshing services to nearly all the farmers of the area. One towed his threshing machine behind a huge steam engine. When this operator was hired to do the threshing there was always a certain amount of concern that an ember would be carried from the firebox of the steam engine to the threshing machine in the barn by the large flat belt. The danger was there, but apparently no fire was ever started at my grandfather's barn because of it. It was quite a sight though, for this young boy, to see the steam engine coming up the road, steam coming out of its boiler stack, and then watching the skill of the operator get the threshing machine into the barn and get ready for the threshing to begin.

The other threshing machine operator towed his machine with a very large gasoline powered tractor – maybe an old Fordson, with steel cleated wheels. The set up was the same for each; however, there was less concern of a fire being started with the gasoline fueled tractor.

Sometimes farmers wanted part of the straw blown to a location within the barn – in grandfather's barn there was an "overshoot" that extended somewhat beyond the mow. When straw was blown into this location a great deal of dust was created. This was especially true if one were working in the section where the straw was being blown. It was often necessary to push the straw around in the "overshoot" otherwise it would bunch up and not be evenly distributed. Yes, I got that job on a couple occasions – primarily because I couldn't do anything else! More experienced persons were in the mow forking the sheaves of grain into the threshing machine the correct way and at the proper rate. And, at that time I wasn't strong enough to carry the threshed grain to the granary. That job would come later.

When a straw stack was wanted outside the barn the blower from the threshing machine was extended through a door or window and the straw was directed to the location desired. This cut down on much of the dust inside the barn

I remember, well, those huge dinners, too, that were prepared for the threshers. Large plates of ham, chicken, or some other meat, corn on the cob in never ending quantities, large dishes of green beans, mashed or fried potatoes, pies, cakes, iced tea or lemonade nobody counted calories!

Homer and I Sampled an Adult Beverage

Not only was the spring house the source of wonderful drinking water, but part of it was a cooling facility for milk, butter milk, cream, butter, pies, or anything else from the kitchen that required a constant cool temperature. It was also a place where soft drinks could be placed to cool, as well as adult beverages.

My cousin, Homer Fischer, and I discovered, one hot day, that our grandfather kept his beer there. Homer was a couple years older than I – he was a little over eight years old and I was about six. We had gone into the spring house to get a drink of water when we saw the capped bottle resting on a stone so that just the top of the bottle was above the water level. There was a bottle opener hanging on the wall – Homer saw it, so did I. "Let's open that bottle and take a drink," Homer said. I didn't protest! The cap was removed from the bottle; Homer took the first swallow and handed the bottle to me. I took a quick, but small swallow – I didn't like it, and gave it back to him. I'm certain that at that moment each of us had a consciousness of guilt because we started wondering out loud how we could keep "grandpap", or our parents from learning what we had done. Homer had the solution. We hadn't drunk very much of the beer – it was just a little low in the neck of the bottle after our imbibing. Homer suggested that we pee in the bottle, bring the beer up to the level it was when we opened it, put the cap back on it and nobody would ever know! We did just that – obviously, we couldn't get the cap back on the top of the bottle as securely as it was when we found it, but we thought it would do. We put the beer bottle back into the water and it looked to us exactly the way it did when we found it. We left the spring house and went about our play.

Our grandfather hadn't reached his seventies, reared six children, been around grandchildren for a while, without having learned a thing or two. Yes, later in the day he went to the spring house – thirsty, I suspect, anticipating drinking that cool beer he had placed in the spring. I guess Homer and I did not realize that a full bottle of beer that was not securely capped would arouse suspicion in the old man. Well, it did! He didn't drink the beer, so he said, and before the day was over there was a complete confession from two little boys. We never did that again.

Spring house on Grandfather's farm

Wisdom from My Elders

My uncles, grandfather, and great uncle, George were my mentors in many ways. In the 1940's, in addition to horses, they also used a tractor. The one I remember was a Farmall 14 – on steel wheels with sharp lugs or cleats on the rear wheels. One day when we were going back to the barn, my Uncle Ted was operating the tractor and out of the blue asked me if I knew how to drive a tractor! I said, "yes" even though I had never driven a tractor before. I had been standing on the draw bar, directly behind the seat where he was sitting. He stopped immediately and told me I could drive to the barn! We exchanged places – he stood on the drawbar and I climbed onto the seat. He said, "Let's go." I pushed in the clutch, pulled the gearshift lever into gear – and released the clutch abruptly! The front end of the tractor left the ground and we lurched forward! I suspect he had anticipated what was going to happen because he had a very good grip on the seat – otherwise he would have landed in the road when I made that old Farmall's front end rise off the ground. "Release the clutch slowly," he said. That was the only comment he made. – and I never made that mistake again.

I don't know why, but Ted seemed to delight in using those big fingers of his to "flip" me behind the ears. Maybe my ears were large and they made a great target, but I remember when I'd be sitting at the table and Ted walked behind me, he couldn't resist giving me a "flip" behind the ears! But, I liked and respected him a lot; I would have done anything he asked me to do.

Another lesson I never forgot I learned from Mike, another uncle. It was the first day of small game hunting season and Mike told me I could go hunting using his .22 caliber rifle. I picked up the rifle and went to a place about a half-mile from my grandfather's house and was tramping through some thickets hoping to see a rabbit. I discovered that the plunger I had to pull in cocking the rifle was too firm for me to pull and still have time to shoot if I saw a rabbit. So I decided to cock the gun and walk around with it ready to shoot!

In a few minutes Mike joined me – he took one quick look at the cocked gun I was carrying and immediately said to me, "Hey, if you want to hunt with me uncock that gun – you never walk around with a cocked gun like that – suppose you fall down, you could shoot yourself." Lesson learned! Never again did I do that.

Grandfather's Farmall 14 tractor

It was also Mike who, after seeing me curled up in bed like a worm, told me if I wanted to grow up to be tall I'd better stretch out and sleep that way. Well, today I doubt very much if how one sleeps has anything to do with adult height, but from an uncle who was over six feet tall and a little boy who didn't want to be short in stature, I certainly heeded his advice!

I believe Mike understood me pretty well when I was a boy – I remember his saying to someone one day – "If hard work ever killed anyone, Billy will live forever." Apparently I had given the impression that I didn't like hard, physical labor. Well, I didn't! – Still don't!!!

My Dog Bing

I have many pleasant memories of Mike – none more so than the fact that he gave me my first dog. No one will ever know how much that dog meant to me! My birthday was a couple days after Mike gave me my puppy. I was supposed to go to my grandfather's farm that day and "hoe" corn. I really didn't want to go. Mom said to me, "Today is your birthday you don't have to work!" Actually, my reluctance to hoe corn that day had nothing to do with my birthday – I wanted to play with my dog! And I did!!! I named him Bingo – but always called him Bing. I thought he was about the prettiest, smartest, friendliest dog that ever lived. His mother was a beagle – but his father was a large, shaggy yellow and white "shepherd" – probably part border collie. I believe his owner called him Ring. He was a stock dog – but, apparently a dog, Don Juan! He certainly got around! There were probably many dogs in the area that had a distinctive white ring around the neck with a white blaze down the nose! My Bing had all the marking of daddy Ring, but his coat was not shaggy or wooly. He had inherited the short coat of his beagle mother.

Regardless of his mixed lineage I loved that dog. I spent hours playing with him – he would sit on a chair, hold a pipe in his mouth, shake hands with me – I even taught him to carry firewood to our porch. Sometimes he'd decide to take an evening off – I'd call and call for him – but no Bing! I would worry that he might never come back, maybe he had been hit by a car, could someone have stolen him?(not likely) but, in the morning he would be on the porch, his coat wet, dirty, burrs on his legs – I was very happy to see him, I quickly forgave him for his adventures of the previous night.

Bing lived to quite an advanced age for a dog. I graduated from high school, spent time in the military, and it wasn't until my second year in college that I got a letter from my mother telling me that Bing had died. She and a friend buried him in the pines that grew a short distance from our house.

My dog Bing and my two sisters

That mongrel dog adventured with me through every book I ever read in which there was a dog hero. He was White Fang, and when I read another of Jack London's books, *Call of the Wild* he morphed into Buck! When I read, *Bob, Son of Battle*, Bing assumed the identity of the dog in that book and he had all the characteristics of Lassie, in *Lassie Come Home*. I have had many dogs since Mike gave me that soft, cuddly little brownish yellow dog that I named Bing, but none left me with as many memories as my Bing. Kipling was right when he said, "Never give your heart to a dog

An Uncle's Prediction

I had another uncle, Leo, who would chide me about being short when I grew up – one day we were on a wagon, pulled by a couple horses, and came to a section of the public road where a road crew was working. One of the workmen, wearing khaki trousers and being all of five feet tall on his tip toes and just about as broad, was crossing the road a short distance in front of us. He walked with a kind of waddle! This uncle, something of a jokester, said to me, "There, Billy, that's how you'll look when you grow up." To a ten year old who wanted to be as tall as his uncles – I now had a great incentive to eat everything on my plate and, yes, stretch out every night when I crawled into bed!

This uncle never lost his sense of humor. When he was in his mid 80's, living by himself after his wife had passed away, I stopped to see him the day after the Republicans had gained control of congress. He was receiving "Meals on Wheels" and his lunch had just been delivered. He looked at it and noted that there was only a half banana. He looked at me and with a smile on his face said, "You can tell the Republicans are in control now, can't you – look, they've already cut the bananas in half!" He lived to be 90 years old – I still miss him.

Lack of Sex Education

I think my grandfather knew how gullible I was and that I believed everything he told me. One year he raised several colts. They were in a field close to our house. I would see them everyday. There was one that I liked very much. One evening my grandfather pointed to the colt I liked and said to me, "Billy, when that colt grows up and has a colt, I'm going to give it to you." Well, that made my day – in fact, many days, yes I remembered that promise for the next couple years. Imagine my surprise when I finally discovered after two years that the colt I liked – and whose colt would someday be mine, was a male! We had no courses in sex education at my school!!!!

The Amateur Barber

On occasions my grandfather would ask me to cut his hair – I guess I was a last resort. No one else would cut his hair, and everybody was too busy to take him to a barber. And, I agreed to give him a hair cut. One day when I was just about finished – one of my uncles, Bill Fischer, took one look at my tonsorial efforts and said, "Bill, you have his head looking like a peach!" It probably did. We had a pair of hand clippers. I think my dad bought them with the intent of cutting my hair. Only once was he my barber – my guess is that mom served as a protector of any future embarrassment for me. I knew nothing about cutting hair. I can remember cutting my grandfather's hair too high on one side of his head – – then I'd work on the other side trying to match it to the other side. For some reason or other the two sides never matched. That meant I had to go higher and higher until I ran out of hair – he didn't have too much hair on the top of his head to start with – much less when I had finished!

I also "trimmed" my great uncle George's hair once in awhile. I didn't use the clippers too much on him – mostly only the scissors. My efforts on George quite closely resembled a bowl cut! George had a very bushy moustache – he couldn't see too well but he apparently sensed that the moustache needed shaped every so often. He would trim it himself but afterwards one could see "notches" in it – or one side would be shorter than the other. A rather asymmetrical moustache trim. Fortunately, I don't believe the old fellow (he was in his late 70's) ever had one of my haircuts and his own mustache trim at the same time.

My grandfather was born in 1867 and my great Uncle George was born in 1864. They never knew it, but each served as a kind of historical time line for me. While in elementary school when I would read of some historical event that occurred within their life time, I would calculate how old they were at the time of the event and wonder if they had read about it in the newspaper! Specifically, I remember when reading about the 1876 Battle of the Little Big Horn wondering if George or my grandfather talked about it! Did they listen to conversation between and among the Civil War veterans that would have visited in their home when they were boys my age? Did they ever think about "going west" and becoming cowboys during the 1880's and 1890's? Had they read about the Earps – Did they read about the Gun Fight at the OK Corral? I wondered if they had ever heard anyone say, "Remember the Maine" at the outbreak of the Spanish American War. I suspect all those thoughts were simply the imagination of a young boy who, vicariously, shared the adventures of whatever event or episode he happened to be reading about. My grandfather and great uncle were probably too preoccupied at the time of those events with small, everyday incidents in their own lives to pay much attention to what was happening miles and miles away. They probably didn't have access to a weekly paper, certainly not a daily one!

Grandfather and two of his younger sisters

My Great Uncle George Northcraft

The Old Dam

I referred to it as the Old Dam, although in my life time there was no dam there. Years ago there had been, of course. During the ten years or so that I lived within a mile of

Sideling Hill Creek there had always been this old grist mill, referred to by my mother and others, as the Pott's Mill. It took its name from the family from whom my grandfather bought the land on which it was located. Directly behind the structure was that part of the stream that I, and everyone else, referred to as the dam. The mill that I remember was an unpainted structure on land that my grandfather had purchased many years before. By the time he purchased the land on which it stood it no longer functioned as a mill. As a boy I remember being inside the structure and looking at the large timbers close to the roof and seeing what looked like flour dust or residue from grinding grain. I asked questions, too, about the kind of water wheel that might have been used – I was told that the wheel was located underneath the structure.

My grandfather never used the mill for milling purposes; he had other uses for it, however. I remember an old buggy and spring wagon were housed there. And more importantly, part of the structure had been converted into an ice house. Ice was cut from the creek that ran behind the mill or other places nearby where it was accessible and easily transportable to the mill. In preparing for the ice a rather thick layer of sawdust was placed inside the part of the mill that had been converted to an ice house. Then a layer of ice cut into manageable sized blocks was placed on top of the sawdust. This layering continued until the structure could hold no more. The ice remained until quite late into the summer. During June and early July when the family wanted ice they went to the "Old Mill," dug down through the sawdust until ice was located an took out a piece large enough to make a hand cranked freezer or two of home made ice cream or to provide ice for iced tea! One of my memories of looking at the sawdust that covered the ice during the summer months was seeing a large black snake in one corner – apparently enjoying the feel of sawdust on his belly! I didn't disturb him – he liked that spot, I suppose; I saw him there on other visits to the mill!

Directly behind the mill there was a rock ledge that jutted out of the water along the bank—directly behind the mill. There was a slight bend at this point and the water was quite deep. During the afternoon when the sun was at the right angle one could look down into the water and see fish – particularly, small mouth bass swimming up and down the length of the rock ledge. I fished there many times. I used to catch grasshoppers from the nearby fields and use them as bait to catch the bass and blue gills. It was a great place for a ten year old to swim, too. The deepest part was directly off the ledge – within five or six feet of the ledge, however, the water became very shallow and one could easily wade to the far side. I swam there often with a cousin who was a couple years older than I.

Rock ledge overlooking the site that was once part of the grist mill dam.

Falling off a Plow Horse

It was in the field that lay opposite the mill where I had my first experience of falling off a horse. We had recently moved from Pittsburgh, Pennsylvania and for a short time my family lived with my grandparents. My father had grown up on a farm and was used to doing the type work necessary on a farm during that era, He was quite at home behind a plow. I apparently had a great desire to ride horses during that spring following our move from Pittsburgh. On this particular morning my father was going to plow in the field that was opposite the old mill. At some time or other apple trees had been planted in the field but only a couple still remained. The plow – a walk behind plow, had already been taken to the field. He put the harness on the two horses – one was named Kate, the other Nance. Kate was the mother of Nance. Both were very large horses. Kate was white – Nance was gray. He lifted me up on Kate's back – I was four years old – and I gripped the hames as he drove the horses the half mile to the field where he would be plowing. He hitched the horses to the plow and made a round or two. Apparently he was too engrossed in keeping a straight furrow to notice that he was approaching one of the lone apple trees in the field. My horse, Kate, was headed just a little to the left of the tree in front of us. I guess I thought I could duck the limb that Kate lowered her head to miss – but, I didn't duck soon enough. Before I could utter any warning a limb caught my shoulder and side of my face and I was dragged off. My dad immediately stopped the horses, but I had landed right alongside of Kate's right rear hoof! I remember looking up at her belly!!! Dad helped me up and soon determined that I wasn't hurt – only a few scratches on my face. Dad directed the horses to pull the plow a few feet beyond the tree. He stopped them and lifted me up on the back of Kate and continued plowing until it was time to go to the house for "dinner". – today we'd call it lunch!

My Ride on Old Jack

"Old Jack" was a mule – not a young, frisky one, but one who had been around for many years. I, on the other hand, a young six year old who loved to ride horse back – or, mule back, in this case. Maybe it was my fixation with cowboys, I don't know – but I liked cowboy songs, cowboy hats and I associated riding horses with cowboys! The barn had burned on our farm a short time before we moved on it. The first summer after our move to the farm, construction of the new barn began. My uncle, Mike, knew where there was a very large wooden plank that he had seen along Sideling Hill Creek. Apparently it had been carried there by the high water in the spring. The carpenters had evidently suggested the need for such a piece of timber in their construction. Mike told the workmen about this wooden plank and said he would take "Old Jack" and bring it to the site. I seized the opportunity to tag along with him when he went to the barn on my grandfather's place to get "Old Jack." Mike put the harness on the old mule and lifted me up on his back and told me I could ride him! I sat on the mule's back, something like an oversized horse fly, gripping the hames, while Mike led "Old Jack" the one half to three quarters of a mile to where the wooden plank was. He led the mule a short distance down the dirt road until he came to the gate that opened into the rather long creek bottom field over which we would travel until we came to the plank. We reached the wooden plank apparently at one time it had been a part of a wooden bridge that had been washed away from its original location some miles upstream by a spring flood. I remained on the mule's back while he placed a heavy log chain under and around the end of the plank. Then he lifted the ring that was connected to each trace chain off the hames and connected the chains to a singletree that he had carried while leading Jack from the barn to this site. In a minute or so "Old Jack" was connected to the plank and we were ready to head back to the building site. We started back towards the gate; Mike wasn't leading the mule he was walking behind us. Mike was a young fellow and perhaps his mind was occupied with thoughts much more important than the kid on the mule in front of him! Suddenly, that old mule came to life. – Perhaps he realized that the small figure riding his back was something less than authoritarian. He started trotting, than galloping – and I'm holding on to those hames with all the strength my hands could summon, additionally my legs are cramped around his sides like two pieces of spring steel. Despite Mike's calling, "Whoa, Jack, Whoa," Jack is hell bent for the gate at the far end of the field. I am absolutely scared to death. Perhaps Mike thought I was smart enough to pull back on the reins attached to the bit in the mule's mouth to stop or slow him. But, I was so petrified with fear that my survival was linked to how tightly my hands would clamp the top of those hames! – I never thought of that black leather strap that was connected to the bit in Jack's mouth. Old Jack hadn't lived all those years without learning something; he probably sensed that he had a rider on his back that was absolutely powerless to thwart his desire to get back to the barn as quickly as possible. Old Jack didn't slow up one bit until his head was thrust over the gate separating him from the road that led to the barn!

In a couple of minutes Mike arrived at the gate, with a smile on his face, "That was quite a ride, wasn't it", he said! "Get me off him," I replied, "I'll walk home."

I don't know whatever happened to the mule, I guess my grandfather sold or gave him away. There is one thing, though, of which I am certain, I never rode that mule again.

Hoeing Corn

A few years later with my younger sister, I would be back in the field beside the old mill – I wouldn't be on a horse this time, but rather, my sister and I had hoes in our hands, hoeing weeds out of the corn for our grandfather. My grandfather seemed to think that corn grew better if someone chopped the weeds from between the rows and between the stocks of corn in the rows. Well, each summer until I was strong enough to use the cultivator or a three shovel plow pulled behind a horse, I hoed corn. Sometimes it was by myself, sometimes with my grandfather and his brother, George. It was my younger sister,

Agnes, however, that I remember as my working partner in this field in front of the old mill. Part of this ground, especially that directly in front of the mill, was extremely stony. It was quite difficult to cut out the weeds when the broad hoes we were using often struck the stones and bounced off them without ever entering the soil. This extremely rocky section, however, was concentrated only in this one area. After getting past this section the rest of the row was not too difficult to hoe. Perhaps this part of the field may have been flooded from time to time leaving a deposit of the flat stones that were very much like those found along the shore-line of the creek. Our grandfather agreed to pay us ten cents a row – not too bad, I suppose, until you consider that the rows were nearly a quarter mile long and that one section was extremely stony – we didn't make much money! I do remember, though, how I spent my money that summer. We hoed corn in this field from the middle of June to the early part of July. My birthday was on the Fourth of July – I spent my money for fireworks – a couple packs of those small (don't remember what they were called), but you lit the fuse and tossed them quickly to the ground and listened to the "bang", some rockets, something called cherry bombs, I remember lighting these and dropping them off the Sideling Hill Bridge into the water expecting to see an explosion, but usually the water would drench the lighted fuse and the cherry bombs sank to the bottom, or they floated downstream, without an explosion. Then there were Roman Candles. I liked these; you could hold them in your hand, light the fuse, and point them toward the sky and several balls of different colors, one after another, would soar into the black sky and burn out before coming back to the ground.

Two Boys Are Worth a Half Boy

One day I was asked to work in a corn field that was referred to as the "saw briar bottom", so named, I suppose because of the abundance of a particular nasty vine that had spines on its stem and would cling to your clothes or scratch the skin if it came into contact with either. The field was bordered on one edge by Sideling Hill Creek – and a rather nice pond had formed where the creek made a slight bend close to the field. For whatever reason, my cousin, Homer, went with me that day – I believe he took a hoe along, too. It was a hot day and the water was much more inviting than chopping weeds from the middle of a corn row or weeds that grew between stocks of corn!

As I remember we would work a short while and then rest beneath a rather large tree, and then we'd swim for a much longer time. Actually, we got very little work done that afternoon! But, wow, did we have a lot of fun! It was pretty obvious to my uncles and grandfather that our work output was very slight. That observation prompted one of my uncles to remark, "When you send two boys out to do a job, you have only a half boy!"

The Old Mill Disappears

Sometime during the late 1940's or 1950's my uncle, who now owned the property where the old mill stood, burned it, or had it torn down. It had completely outlived its usefulness – no longer needed as an icehouse, those who used to depend on the icehouse for summer ice now had refrigerators! Besides, imagine the extremely hard work that was involved in cutting ice from the stream, hauling it to the ice house, covering it with saw dust – all this had to be done when the weather was extremely cold! The building was deteriorating very badly and – no longer needed for anything. So, after many, many years it met a deliberate demise! Today, a metal pole barn, erected by my grandfather's grandson and great grandson stands very close to where the mill stood and a herd of cattle graze nearby. But, some things don't change – the rock ledge behind where the mill once stood is still there and on a clear day when the sun is in the right position overhead, a small boy could still look down into the water and see smallmouth bass and sunfish swimming the length of the pool. And, I'm certain that today the water would feel just as refreshing to a ten year old on a hot summer day as it did 70 years ago.

A Sledding Collision with Grandfather

It was a week or so before Christmas and on this particular night my family was visiting with my maternal grandparents. We lived about a mile from them and, since we did not have a car at this time, we would often walk "down home" as my mother referred to my grandparents' place, to visit. On this evening I was back in the "parlor" probably playing with the rather large, pump organ, which no one in the family ever played, or maybe looking at stereographs through the stereoscope that was kept there, when for somc rcason or other I looked underneath the leather, upholstered fainting couch that was placed along the wall. And, there it was! The new sled that I was really hoping to get for Christmas. I couldn't conceal my glee – I ran to the kitchen and practically shouted to my mother that I had found "my sled". There was no way that I was going to wait 'til Christmas to get that sled! After some pleading with my mother – I was allowed to receive my Christmas gift early. It wasn't a very big sled – probably 32 inches long; it had been ordered from the Sears Roebuck catalog and it had an arrow painted on the center top slat of the sled, and the words, Flying Arrow, also appeared in large letters. The runners and braces were painted bright red. I was six years old and that was the most beautiful sled I had ever seen. I carried it home that night – there was no snow on the ground.

I did not have to wait too long, however, for the first snowfall. And as soon as the ground was white I was coasting down every hill around our house. It was one of those winters when the snow seemed to arrive early and, in the mind of a six year old at least, it never seemed to leave –

every day there was snow on the ground and those down hill sled paths seemed to get slicker and slicker. One such sledding path or run was at my grandparents. There was quite a slope between my grandparents' house and their pigpen. I had tramped the snow down on this run until it was very tightly packed. During the afternoon the snow softened a bit because the slope faced the southwest. Late in the afternoon the soft, slushy snow froze and the sledding was especially fast on this particular path. About three quarters the way down the sled run it crossed a path that led to the pigpen, the path followed when my grandfather would carry feed to his pigs.

The sun had gone down and soon it would be too dark to sled-ride, but I wanted to take one more ride before going into the house. I went to the top of the slope and with a great "belly slam" I started down. I thought I saw a figure walking up the path toward the pigpen, but, unfortunately, disregarded it. That is, until I realized I was on a perfect collision course with the figure walking up the path toward the pigpen. The figure happened to be my grandfather—carrying a burlap sack full of corn on his right shoulder. He couldn't see me because the sack of corn on his right shoulder blocked his view of my descent! There was no way that I could stop or even slow down – all I could do was call, "Watch Out"! But, if he heard my call he didn't have time to react – because the front of my sled collided with his heavy rubber boots just above the ankles! In an instant grand pap was on the ground, I was rolling down the hill and the corn was strewn all over the hill side. I stopped rolling, but before I could get up I heard grandpap using words I'd never heard before! I figured he was pretty mad! So I didn't offer to help him pick up all those ears of corn that were all over the place. My only defense before running toward the house was a feeble, "I called, Watch Out!" At that moment, I don't believe he was very impressed with my defense.

Later that night I heard him laughing about the incident – he was saying to my dad, "I didn't know Billy was sled riding on that hill – until he ran into me!" As I remember, I tried to stay away from grand pap (I always called him grand pap – grandfather would have been much too formal!) for the next several days. As a six year old I guess I didn't have a very good understanding of the "rules of the road". But, intuitively, I knew that grand pap still remembered that I had run into him—and, I hadn't forgotten some of those "new" words I heard when he was getting back on his feet after our collision! Anyway, it was a great sled – it survived six years of heavy winter use by me and several years more by my younger brother and sisters. Many, many years after it had been "retired" by everyone I found it underneath an outbuilding on my parents' farm. I retrieved it and took it to a little shop that I had at my home. I replaced some broken slats on the top of it, repaired broken braces, and planned to place it on my porch at Christmas time loaded down with boxes wrapped in brightly colored seasonal wrapping paper.

Grandfather – well, I'm certain he forgave me for my "reckless" sled ride as a six year old. During the summer months – probably starting the summer after my sledding accident, he "hired" me to hoe corn with him. Sometimes when the rows were extremely long he'd pay me ten cents a row! Other times, an equivalent amount – but probably not more than fifty cents for as long as we would work. And, there were times when he simply forgot to pay me anything! The sun was very hot in those cornfields, and grand pap would say, "Time for a rest and a drink of water". I never disagreed! Grand pap was always five or six feet ahead of me in his row – somehow or other I never could pass him. On occasion I would miss the weed I was trying to remove and chop off a sturdy stock of corn. Immediately I would pull dirt around it – thinking it wouldn't be noticed by him on our return across the field. But, when we would reach the spot of my "fatally wounded chopped off stock," which by this time had wilted because of the hot sun, he'd say, "I wonder what happened to that one?" (As though he didn't know!)

Many times when I was still in elementary school instead of walking to my home I would walk to my grandparents' home. I could always expect a bit of "after school" teaching from grandfather. For a person who did not have very much formal education, his arithmetical skills were great. His was a practical use of arithmetic – he had operated a general store for many years, and, additionally, transported his farm produce – butter, eggs, meat, vegetables to Cumberland, Maryland, nearly thirty miles away. Not by a motorized vehicle, but rather in a wagon covered with a canvas and pulled by four horses. Each week he visited his customers supplying them with his farm fresh products. So his questions to me related to the buying and selling of farm products – "If I buy three dozen eggs from a farmer for 25 cents a dozen how much do I have to sell them for if I want to make a profit of 75 cents?" Or, "If I break three eggs and I am selling my eggs at 25 cents a dozen, how much money have I lost by breaking those three eggs?" These and similar questions were standard fare when I visited grandfather after school.

The sled

As time went by and I entered my teenage years I spent much less time with my grandparents. Eventually, I entered the US Navy and grandfather was someone that I saw maybe once a year. It was, however, while I was still in the Navy and during the Christmas season that I got a call from my mother telling me that my grandfather had passed away. He enriched my boyhood days much more than he ever realized – And most importantly, gave me a reservoir of memories that deal with a time, a place and a personality that today give me much joy as I reflect on them. And the sled, each time I look at it I think of grand pap and that late afternoon collision we had.

Chapter 7

Sideling Hill Creek

Description

As far as I know Sidling Hill Creek has no truly historical significance. No important battles were fought over it, no treaties were signed on its banks, in fact, outside of the townships through which it flows in Bedford and Fulton Counties, Pennsylvania – and Alleghany and Washington Counties, Maryland where it empties into the Potomac River, probably few people have ever heard of it. I write about it because I spent about 11 years of my boyhood on a small farm in Fulton County within a mile of it. The creek bisected my grandfather's farm, whose land bordered the farm on which I lived.

My mother was born on my grandfather's farm and my father was born and lived his boyhood days on a farm that bordered one of two main branches of the creek, near Purcell, locally known as Little Creek.

All my boyhood friends and I fished and swam in Sideling Hill Creek.. In the winter when it froze over and the ice was clear I would walk on it and look at the fish below. I didn't have ice skates, but on my sled I could glide from one end of the long ponds to the other with what seemed to a ten year old to be frightening speed – being careful, of course to steer closer to the shore before coming to the riffles at the upper or lower end of the ponds where the water was not frozen!

The watershed, located in the Ridge and Valley section of Pennsylvania and Maryland, is beautiful, and, rather pristine. Rather unspoiled, I think. I suspect it represents today what many small streams in much of rural Pennsylvania used to be like. Small spring fed tributaries, bolstered by run off from the many steep hills, increase the creek's flow, especially in the spring of the year. These small tributaries represent small watersheds. Some of these streams provide spawning grounds for migrating fish in the spring – particularly, for what we called "suckers," bottom feeders that sometimes become trapped in small pools later in the spring and summer when the flow of water is slight, to become food for raccoons and targets for young boys with a fishing rod or gig! The two tributaries with which I was most familiar were Crooked Run and Trough Run. Crooked Run begins in Mann Township, Bedford County and empties into Sideling Hill Creek in Union Township, Fulton County shortly after flowing out of Mann Township. The source of the other tributary, called Trough Run, is entirely in Union Township, Fulton County. The ridges on either side of Trough Run are quite steep. The run off from winter snow results in a heavy flow during the spring; however, by mid to late summer there is little if any water flow. I remember crossing Trough Run one very dark night, under almost blizzard conditions. I was in high school and the basketball team had played a game some distance from my home school. The school bus that had taken the team to the school site where the game was played later brought the team back to our home school after the game was over. Unfortunately, an unexpected snow storm had begun before the game ended and the roads were quickly becoming very difficult for safe driving. When we arrived at our home school a couple of us discovered that we had no transportation to our homes! So, there was but one thing for us to do and that was to begin walking the distance of 12 or 15 miles. It was a long, difficult walk under those snowy conditions.

When I came to within about four miles from my home I had a decision to make. I could walk down the side of a steep ridge and cross Trough Run and walk up an old dug road and be rather close to my home – or follow the main roads for nearly four miles! I opted to cross Trough Run! Well, it wasn't too difficult walking down the slope and woods to get to Trough Run, the difficulty would be in crossing it! As noted above it was snowing very hard – probably four or five inches on the ground. I was not wearing any kind of rubber overshoes or boots. My feet were cold and wet. I knew there was no bridge across the Run where I wanted to cross, but I knew that several years before a large tree had blown across the little stream; now it looked like a large log spanning the small gorge. Earlier that year I had walked from one bank to the other on this log. The big problem on this night; however, was that it was snowing, very dark and I didn't know exactly where the log was. I discovered I was too far upstream from my "bridge" so I began moving slowly downstream until I practically stumbled over it. Since it was pitch dark along the stream I knew I couldn't walk across the log. I got on my hands and knees and crawled across it – there was a good flow this time of year, I could hear the sound of water running over the rocky stream bed. I had little trouble finding the old dug road. In another half hour I was home – wet and uncomfortable, certainly glad to get my wet clothes off and get ready for bed. After all, in a couple hours I would have to get out of bed, go to the barn and milk the cows, and then get ready to catch the school bus!

No major industrial sites are located within the Sideling Hill water shed – small farming operations still predominate. The stream remains largely unpolluted. One can still find fresh water mussels along the stream bed. The Western Pennsylvania Conservancy has long been interested in the Sideling Hill Watershed. The Conservancy owns more than 300 acres of land in the watershed and remains active in preserving it unique biodiversity. The goal of this organization is to work with the communities within the watershed in such ways as to protect "this special place" and at the same time promote economic and social growth of the population living there. The Pennsylvania Department of

Environmental Protection has designated the stream of Exceptional Value.

Many residents today do not earn their livelihood working the land as was formerly the case. Rather, they work in nearby towns in Pennsylvania and Maryland.

Fresh water mussels shells can still be found along the creek

Sideling Hill Creek has it origin where two primary sources merge – just below a small hamlet known as Purcell in Mann Township, Bedford County The two streams, locally known as Big Creek and Little Creek. Little Creek is east of Big Creek. Sideling Hill Creek flows in a southerly direction through Mann Township, Bedford County, enters Union Township, Fulton County near the Maryland line and then after meandering through a rather wooded and hilly section forming the boundary between Washington and Allegany Counties in Maryland, it flows under the C&O aqua duct into the Potomac River.

I have never done it, but I have always thought the creek – from its source, to where it empties into the Potomac River, would be an excellent canoe journey in early spring when the water flow would be sufficient to carry a canoe through the many riffles and shallow areas of the stream. The scenery would be terrific!

An Early Morning Fishing Trip

It was an hour or so before day light when I got up – quite sleepy, but I had planned to fish a long stretch of Sideling Hill Creek that morning. I would start my fishing journey at Sideling Hill Creek Bridge and work my way upstream as far as the dam at Silver Mills – we referred to the dam as the Akers's dam.

The day before I had seined for minnows in Crooked Run and I had them in a metal container that had been immersed overnight in a spring below our barn. It would take me about 25 minutes to get to the bridge and then I'd begin fishing. I had a small minnow bucket slung over my shoulder and my fishing rod in my hand – on my belt I had hooked a bait carrier in which I had an ample supply of worms – big and little ones. In my pocket I carried a metal, chain stringer. I was prepared! I set off for the bridge and actually made better time than I had expected – it was still quite dark, probably would not be light for another 45 minutes. I more or less felt my way down to the edge of the water at the bridge The first place I wanted to fish was directly upstream from the bridge. I really didn't expect to catch anything here this morning – I never had very good luck here. However, a couple hundred yard up stream there was a stretch of water just below what we called the "Old Dam" where I had seen some small mouth bass and many sunfish. However, to fish that pool I had to cross the creek and fish from the opposite side. In that particular pond there were large rocks in the middle. But it's still not daylight and I didn't know how I would be able to see those rocks where I wanted to toss my bait. First, however, I had to get across the creek. There were riffles where I was then located so I didn't think I'd have any problems crossing. I was wearing an old pair of trousers and had on an old pair of shoes. My feet were already wet and my trousers were wet about half way to my knees. I started across the riffles – I was certain there where no deep holes at this point, so I proceeded to cross without difficulty. Now,

I'm almost to the spot where I wanted to throw my bait – I had threaded a rather large night crawler on my hook, a few more feet and I knew I'd be at the right location! But, I guess I had forgotten about a large, smooth sloping rock that was barely covered with water near the shore line, and then sloped to nearly the center of the creek where the water was probably three feet deep! I stepped forward with my left foot and in the next instant I'm sliding on my thigh toward the deeper water – from maybe 6 inches to nearly three feet! Within a couple seconds I'm on my side in the water, nearly immersed, holding my rod with my right hand and flailing with my left arm – trying, I guess, to find something to grasp so that I could get up! Well, I did get up – but I was soaked. I didn't loose my minnow bucket, but I didn't know whether there was still anything in it! I soon discovered there was not! I was cold, wet, and shivering – the thought occurred to me, "Why don't you go home?" No, I had thought about this trip for too long; I was not going home, besides the sun would soon be up and I'd be warm again. I made several cast into the area where the large rocks were – but with all the commotion that I had just caused, fish that might have been there were probably in hiding. So I moved on.

By now it was light enough that I no longer had to stumble along the bank. I worked my way upstream to the tail end of a large pond – we used to refer to the place as "Mandy's Bottom" – named for the woman who owned the bottom land that was alongside the pond. I made a long cast upstream and as soon as the over sized night crawler bait hit the water there was an immediate swirl in the water where the bait landed. It was a pike, I thought. Actually, what we always called "pike" were really chain pickerel. I reeled the fish in and, sure enough, it was a rather large pickerel. Carefully, I removed the hook from his mouth – I say carefully, because pickerel have a mouthful of very sharp teeth, I put him on my stringer, hooked the other end of the stringer on a belt loop of my trousers and moved on.

By now it's fairly light and after catching my first fish, my mind was no longer occupied with "being cold and wet". My next desired location was a very deep and long pond that we always called the "Beaver Pond". In order to get there as quickly as possible I had to pass by several good fishing spots – but, I told myself that I'd stop at those places on my way back later in the day. After several minutes walking I came to the Beaver Pond. The spot I wanted to go to was shaded by several large trees along the bank. The sun had not yet penetrated the overhang of trees along this part of the stream, because of this the opposite bank was not very well lighted. This particular location of the creek had pleasant memories for me. This was a favorite spot of my Uncle Ross. He liked to come here and fish at night. Frankly, I never enjoyed fishing after dark. Ross would have his kerosene lantern and a flashlight, plus a container in which he had something to drink; he was content to fish until very late at night – usually he didn't want to leave until he had drunk all of whatever liquid he had brought with him. I was usually ready to leave much earlier; I had to get up early the next morning and go to school!

Another memory I had of this fishing spot was the late afternoon I was fishing there and took an unexpected dip in the water. I had noticed a pile of what I thought was "driftwood" below the low bank on which I was standing. Without giving the pile of wood very much thought I stepped on it – thinking I could get a better cast to a certain location in the pond. I stepped onto the pile and immediately my leg went right through it into the water. I was able to fall backward onto the bank before falling into the water. Only one leg was wet. Shortly thereafter an old friend, Bill Karns and his father, came to the same location to fish. Bill looked at my wet leg and asked me if I'd fallen into the water. I told him what had happened. He looked at the driftwood I had stepped on and told me I had stepped on top of a snapping turtle nest! His father, an older gentlemen in his 70's suggested that the best thing anyone could do when stepping on such a pile of driftwood was to lunge forward into deeper water and then swim back to shore. Guess I was lucky that I caught myself before falling farther into the pile of brush. I don't know if Bill was correct when he identified the pile of "driftwood" as a snapping turtle nest or not, I do know that I was very careful in the future never to step off the bank onto a pile of brush that was on top of the water!.

On the spot where I now stood I could look across the water and see a very large rock that appeared to jut out of the cliff and extend almost to the water's edge. There was a smooth bank beneath the rock that gently sloped to the water. While standing there looking across the pond – perhaps a little over a hundred feet, I saw two small heads moving upstream. I didn't know what I was looking at until each made a sharp turn in the water and headed for the sloping bank underneath the large outcropping rock. As they moved out of the water and up the bank I could see the broad tail and knew immediately that they were beavers. I had never seen beavers before – I later learned that they were "bank beavers" meaning that they did not build dams; instead, they burrow from under water into the bank and build their home there. The "Beaver Pond" on Sideling Hill Creek – where I was that morning – was ideally suited for bank beavers. The water was deep providing storage for their winter supply of small saplings, twigs, and small sections of trees.

After that morning's experience with beavers – I noted on succeeding fishing trips evidence of beaver activity in different sections of the land bordering the creek. Small trees, for example that had been cut by beavers. From doing a little research on the habits of beavers I learned that they preferred to eat the bark and inner bark of aspen, birch, maple and that they could cut down a 4 to 6 inch tree in about 3 minutes However, despite their preference for eating the bark of certain species of trees, I discovered that in the absence of favorites they will, if need be, eat the bark from other species as well. I watched the beavers under the large rock for a few minutes and then they moved down to the water, swam a short distance and suddenly disappeared – both executed a dive at the same time. I fished at this location for perhaps 30 minutes without any success and then decided to move on to another location – farther up stream to The Silver Mill's Dam.

In earlier years the dam furnished water power for a grist mill that was located a relatively short distance from the dam. As a small boy I remembered looking at the mill race and noted how clean it looked – free of rubble. The mill did not have an over-shot wheel as one often sees on old grist mills, rather, it was located beneath the structure. These types of wheels were not as efficient as those mounted vertically on the exterior of a mill. After moving beneath the mill, turning the turbine, the water then flowed onward through the race and back into the creek. A sluice gate allowed the water to flow through the race and activate the power wheel. A large gear was powered by the water wheel – whether under the mill or on the exterior, which in turn meshed with a smaller gear that turned the top grind stone. The stone could weigh as much or more than 1000 pounds. There were a pair of stones, each was grooved with many groves running from the center to the outer perimeter. Grain entered the stones through the center hole and, because of the top stone's rotation, moved from the center to the outer rim. The bottom stone was stationary – but also grooved. As the top stone rotated, the action with respect to the bottom one was a scissors action. The grooves were deeper closer to the center of the stones than nearer the edges. As the grain moved towards the edge, the grain was ground finer and finer by coming in contact with the edge of the groove. The closeness of the stones together determined the fineness of the grind. The stones were not allowed to touch each other. The grooves in the stones not only helped to move the flour or meal to the exterior, but also served to keep the stones somewhat cool, because of the airflow through them. Fire was always a danger in a mill – if the stones became overheated, there was a danger of certain types of flour exploding resulting in a fire that would consume the mill.

Even the lanterns used in a mill were shielded with a heavy wire grid to help prevent accidental breaking of the globe and exposing the dust to possible explosion by coming in contact with the lighted lantern wick.

Mill lantern

There was a great deal of skill required by a successful miller. He had to know just how close together the stones were in order to grind different types of meal or flour.

The water was quite low in the dam this morning; I fished there a few minutes without any success and decided to go downstream and visit those spots that I had skipped earlier in the morning. I recall looking at a beautiful "cucumber tree," a relative of the magnolia family, its leaves were large and had a dark green, glossy appearance to them – later in the summer I went back to see it again, there were many little "cucumbers" (seeds) on it! That same morning I saw also a beautiful "hog nose" snake – he puffed a little at me and when I poked him gently with a stick, he rolled over pretending he was dead, I guess! I walked on.

In my rush to get to the Beaver Pond and the Silver Mill's Dam I had bi-passed some places where I wanted to fish. I quickly walked back to the lower end of the Beaver Pond. Beginning there I recalled that there were a number of small holes – some below fast riffles – I was certain I would catch some rock bass or goggle eyes as we called them. I did. In fact, quite a number of them. I continued down stream to a spot I remembered from a previous visit to this part of

Sideling Hill Creek. On my right side was a steep cliff—the water had a deep green cast to it. I had a non-descript, small bass artificial lure in a small case I carried in my pocket. I noted a partially submerged log in the water. Near the edge of the pool the log was clearly visible, but it seemed to disappear in the deeper water in the center of the stream. I thought to myself – a good place for a smallmouth bass! I tied the lure on my line and cast it downstream toward the submerged log and began my retrieve. Suddenly, the line was taut and the tip of my rod bent more than I had ever seen it bend before. Hey, I have a real lunker on this time, I thought. I lifted the rod and put considerable pressure on it. I could feel the power and strength of the fish as he fought in the deep water. Suddenly, I noticed the rod was still bent, but I felt no struggle as I had only a few seconds ago. That damn log, I thought, – bet the fish has wrapped itself around a snag on it! I waited a minute or so thinking the fish would resume previous activity. Well, it didn't. I really wanted to see that fish!

I took off my clothes – down to my shorts, and waded as far as I could and then started swimming into the deeper water. When I was a few feet from the log I dived and swam under water to the spot where I thought the fish would be. I didn't find that big lunker, but there was my lure – near the bottom of that log about ten inches above the stream bed. I retrieved it, surfaced, and swam back across the deeper water and then waded to the shore where I had taken off my clothes. I was disappointed that I did not get to see the fish. But, I certainly got cooled off, though! – I waited a half hour or so until my shorts were nearly dry! Put my clothes back on and started my walk home – enough fishing for the day.

In my walk home I went by the little "island" pond – that's what we called those little pools of water that were separated from the main stream – during periods of stream flooding; water from the creek would fill some of these depression – perhaps, too, they were fed by springs – the ponds always seemed to have about the same amount of water in them.

This particular pond always had pickerel in it – as boys we called them pike! This was the pond that my cousin, Homer Fischer, and I decided to drain one afternoon. We had seen the "pike" in there and tried to catch them with our assortment of baits – consisting of minnows, lures and worms! The fish were much smarter than we were – No doubt they had seen us and had taken cover in the many hiding places in the pond. We made cast after cast using everything we had that we thought would be enticing to the fish! Absolutely no success.

Homer said to me, "Let's drain this pond." I agreed. We went to the lower end of the pool – only a very small amount of water was leaving it. There was a channel that veered to the right back into the creek. "How are we going to drain the water out of here," I asked Homer. He had the answer – already he had a pretty stout stick and was trying to gouge a miniature ditch in the slight channel that was already there. I, too, found a piece of a fallen tree limb and joined him in making the "ditch" deeper and wider. It was obvious to us that the water was flowing a bit faster now than before – but, it was also clear to us by now that our "ditch" was going to have to be much deeper than we could make it with our pointed sticks in order to get to those pike! After an hour or so of this kind of work our interest waned – and we went home! And, the "pike" continued to swim in their island pond.

I Took My Little Brother Fishing

By the time my brother was old enough to fish I had been away from home for a few years. However, one Saturday when I was visited my parents I decided to take him fishing. We dug the worms, put them in a can and headed off toward Sideling Hill Creek and the fishing hole of our choice. I believe it was at the location we called the "Old Dam." In order to get to the rock ledge alongside the water where we planned to fish we had to go through some thick underbrush and climb down a somewhat steep bank – steep at least for a six year old! Finally we are standing on the rock ledge – the water looked very promising – both of us expecting to catch blue gills and possibly a nice size smallmouth bass. I had been carrying both rods and was now in the process of tying on a hook and putting a small sinker on his line. Now, I am ready to put a worm on the hook and have him drop it over the rock ledge and catch the first fish (I was more interested in his catching fish than I was in my own fishing – I'd had more than my share fishing this very spot many years earlier)

"Okay, Buddy", I said, "We're ready to catch fish – give me the baits?" Silence! I looked in his direction, and said again, "Give me the worms." A rather pained expression greeted me. " I don't have them," he said. "What, I replied, where are they?" A very feeble, "I lost them," was the answer. We looked briefly in the thickets that we had just come through – but didn't find them. I don't know why we didn't go home, get more bait and come back. Perhaps the enthusiasm for fishing that day was lost – or maybe there just wasn't time. Anyway, we went home – the bright side, we would not have to clean fish that evening!!!!

The New Fishing Line - and Uncle Bill

It was a steamy, hot day in early summer. The sun appeared to be shining through a thick haze. I stood outside of a small country church making small talk with a boyhood friend that I had not seen for many years. The occasion was the funeral service of an uncle of mine. Three days before I had received a letter from my mother telling me that my uncle—an uncle by marriage, had died. My Uncle Bill Fischer was a somewhat complex person – he could be the kindest, most considerate individual on some occasions, and be an irascible, argumentative, quick tempered person at other times. But, he was always good to me.

Soon the service began and those friends and relatives who had not yet entered the church did so. I sat in a pew on the right side of the church, directly behind my uncle's youngest grandson; I thought how much that little one resembled his grandfather.

As the minister began his eulogy, my mind wandered back to a long ago time when I was a six or seven year old. I was visiting at my uncle's house that morning and for some reason or other he needed to go the store. At the time he was living in the Pott's House, my grandfather owned it. It was an old unpainted farm house. My aunt was a school teacher and her family moved quite frequently to be as close as possible to whatever school she was assigned. They had one son, named Homer, about three years older than I was. He and I played a lot together, but on this particular morning he was not at home. When Bill needed to go to the store – he meant Barnes's Store – about a mile or so up the road from where he lived. It was a typical country store carrying everything from groceries to eye glasses. Local farmers could buy hardware items, leather for harness repairs, shoes, dry goods and just about anything else that was needed in the home or on the farm. My uncle said to me, "Bill, I'm going to the store, want to go along?" One of the reason I liked my uncle was that he called me "Bill". Nearly everyone else called me "Billy". Nor did I ever address him as Uncle Bill it was always, just Bill! I wasted no time in saying yes and I climbed into the front seat of his green, Model A Ford coupe.

We were soon inside the store and while Bill was making his purchase my eyes were glued to the contents of a small display case at the front of the store. I'm still looking when he is ready to leave. He looked at me and said, "Is there something in there you need?" "Oh," I said, "I was just looking at the fishing lines." The fishing lines were coiled on small rectangular pieces of cardboard, green in color and, I believe, each was fifty feet long and cost ten cents. He looked in the direction of the store keeper and said, "Os," his name was Oscar, but everyone called him Os, "This fellow needs a fishing line." Os went behind the display case, reached in and handed me one of the fishing lines. Bill tossed a dime on the counter and we went out to the car.

On the way home, Bill said to me, "You can catch a big one with that line – it's fifteen pound test." As soon as we got to his house he went out to his garden and along the fence were a number of good size shrubs. He came back to me with a pretty sturdy stock from one of the shrubs and said, "Here's your fishing pole!" I soon had the new line wrapped around the end of it. Then he went into the house and came back out with a small safety pin and a pair of pliers. He cut the clip end off the pin and curled what was left into a hook! So, there I had it – a fishing pole, a line and a hook, all set for a fishing adventure.

Later that day I started towards my grandparents' house – less than a mile away. Before leaving, though, I went to an old barn on the property and dug several "fishing worms"—the little red ones that seemed to be very abundant at that site. I put them in a tin Prince Albert tobacco can, with a little dirt on top and set off towards my grandparents' home. I knew that my dad and mother were there that day – my grandparents owned a large farm and much of the land was located on either side of Sideling Hill Creek. On both sides of the creek were small ponds that, as kids, we referred to as being islands. Actually they were depressions a short distance from the stream bed that would fill with water during heavy rains when the stream would overflow its regular channel. Many sunfish were always in those little ponds. They were trapped there and could easily be seen from the edge of the ponds. The route I chose to return to grandfather's house took me past one of these little ponds. The grass was quite short because 15 or 20 cattle pastured in that field. I could walk right up to the edge of the water.

When I looked into the pond, sunfish could be seen swimming everywhere. I put one of the little red worms on my "safety pin" hook and tossed it into the middle of the pond—I had unwound probably 12 to 15 feet of line. Immediately, it was taken by a very aggressive and hungry sunfish! In seconds the fish was airborne – landing 15 feet or so behind me. I repeated the process several times until my hook was no longer a hook; it had pretty well straightened out. I picked up my fish lying behind me on the grass and put them on a slender branch of a small bush – – I had removed all the lateral twigs from the branch excepting the last one – it looked like a y when finished. With my fish on the "stringer" and fishing pole over my shoulder I headed toward my grandparents' house.

My reverie was broken as the minister finished his eulogy, and like so many funeral services of that era, the family and friends were invited to view the body for the last time. The procession of persons passing by the casket took several minutes. Following the viewing the casket was wheeled to the church exit door and the pall bearers carried it to the gravesite in the adjoining cemetery.

As I implied above, Bill could be rather unpredictable. His quick temper was never very far below the surface. He was very competitive and didn't like to be "bested" by anyone. I remember as a fifteen year old I had purchased a 160 pound barbell set. For about six month I had practiced some overhead lifts – especially the "clean and jerk" In this particular lift you bring the weight up to your chest and then, do a split with your legs, and thrust the weight above your head. The barn floor was my gym. I rolled the weights to the front of the barn and proceeded to do a 'clean and jerk" with 160 pounds. Then, in a cocky manner, I said, "Your turn". Bill wasted no time in accepting the challenge. He gripped the barbell and after a good bit of straining, got the weight to his waist., but despite his struggling and covering most of the barn floor, he couldn't get the weight over his head. Bill dropped the weight and headed for the door. He turned to me and, in an irritated manner, said, "By God, there's a slight to that and you know how to do it – let's go out here and find a heavy object and I'll lift more than you can. I agreed that he was stronger than I was. We didn't look for any more objects to lift, though.

Bill's competitive spirit was often displayed behind the wheel of his car. He delighted in seeing how fast he could "top" a certain mountain or long hill – as well as passing some other motorist on the road ahead of him. I always thought that Bill won a lot "races" on those mountains and hills against other drivers who never realized they were in a race! During the early forties, Bill and Doll purchased a farm about a mile up the road from where my parents lived. Each week day about 3:30 pm one could look up the road and see a cloud of dust arising from the rear of a vehicle that was practically flying on the dirt road that ran beside our house. It was nearly dismissal time where his wife taught school; he would be there on time. Bill, Doll, and their son are all gone now, but I still miss them – each of them gave me a lot of memories.

Skipping Stones across the Water

I should have developed a wonderful throwing arm! I loved throwing stones at cans on a post, throwing stones over buildings, or at any spontaneous target I saw, – but I think most of all I liked skipping stones over water. There were many locations along the creek where I could skip stones either directly across a pond or if I were upstream I could throw them downstream and see how far they would skip on top of the water before sinking. Of course, the secret for me was to find a relatively small, flat stone and with a twist of the wrist and a hard throw have the stone land on the water on the flat side and skip; each succeeding skip a little shorter than the preceding one until the stone lost all momentum and sank.

I Broke Through the Ice

I don't remember why I was there – nor can I understand why I wasn't more aware of the danger! There were two large abutments that supported the Sideling Hill Creek bridge. It was a concrete bridge and the abutments were quite large. The main channel of the creek ran between the abutments. On either side of each was a pool of water that normally was little disturbed by the main flow of the creek. On this particular day, I believe it was Sunday afternoon, I was alone simply exploring the creek, I guess! Anyway, I noticed the flow of water in the main channel had no ice, but I noted that the water on either side of the abutments was frozen. I must have had a strong urge to skate across this iced over part of the creek.. It looked solid all the way over to the abutment. I could get a running start – which I thought would enable me to skate the 15 or 20 feet to the abutment. I did just that and in a matter of seconds I was standing on ice along side the abutment at the end of my glide. But, I made one or more steps toward the shore line when I heard the ice crack! The next thing I knew I had broken through the thin ice and I was in water above my waist!

I was frightened, cold and didn't really know how I could get to the edge of the water. I was "iced" in! I knew from having fished this little pool that the water would be much more shallow as I got closer to the edge. But I couldn't move – yes, the ice had a crack in it, and there was a little space around me where I had broken through, but from me to the edge of the shore line there was ice! I started hammering at the ice with my elbows, breaking out pieces of ice that enabled me to slowly make my way to where the water was shallow enough that I could now take high steps and break a path to the edge! Well, I made it – but I have thought about that event quite often since it happened. I hate to think what would have happened if when I had broken through the ice I would have fallen forward rather than remaining upright as I sank to the bottom of the pool. Believe me, it didn't take me very long to go home – I was freezing.

I did, however, learn a great lesson – before venturing out onto ice: make certain it is thick enough to support your body weight!!!!

A Camping Trip

My first camping trip occurred along Sideling Hill Creek several years after my boyhood days. My family and I were visiting my parents that weekend. They lived about a mile from the spot that I thought would be perfect to take my wife and son on our first camping experience. As a boy I had spent a great amount of time near this "perfect spot" I had fished and swum there alone as well as with other boyhood friends. It was truly one of my favorite places along the creek. During the afternoon I had driven to within a quarter mile of the location, carried my tent, boat, and camping gear to my "perfect" spot. My camping gear consisted of an ancient Baker tent, given to me, with no floor or screened front. It had a flap that one could use to close the opening of the tent or by putting poles under it one could have a flap over the doorway. I had two army cots, three cheap inflatable plastic mattresses, an old kerosene lantern, and a small, but new Coleman gasoline camp stove.

I had taken along a boat that I made—modeled after a small Jon boat. The sides, stern and bow were made from one by twelve inch pine boards. The bottom was made from marine grade plywood. I had painted it a dark green color. It was a sturdy enough little boat – but, not the most handsome!

I pitched the tent under a beautiful Hemlock tree that was about a hundred feet from the creek – at a place we called the Katie Hole, named, I suppose after the house wife who had lived in a house (no longer standing)that was located nearby. The creek made a sharp bend in its course at this point –

before flowing along a steep, rocky cliff for the next quarter mile. I had fished and swum there many, many times as a boy. I thought it was a great feat when I would swim from the Katie hole to the next hole – which we called the Beaver hole – a distance of about a quarter mile. A small tributary, called Trough Run emptied into the creek just a few feet upstream where I had pitched my tent. Overall, the site looked like a perfect place to spend a night. But, we didn't spend the entire night there! My mother and younger brother, Leon, had come down to the site to visit us earlier in the evening. We roasted hot dogs, and chatted – I even persuaded my mother to get into my little boat for a brief ride across the stream – she got into the boat, but for her the five minutes that she spent in the boat while I rowed across the rather small pool and back to my launch site were probably the most anxious five minutes of her life! My rowing was rather erratic, the boat rode low in the water and – mom kept reminding me that she couldn't swim. I rowed the little boat back to where mom boarded it and helped her get out – we almost tipped it, but she got out ok without even getting her feet wet.

It was nearly dark when mom and my brother decided to go home. Now, it's just the three of us on our first camping trip. I lit the kerosene lantern and the smell of the stale kerosene was not pleasant! The mosquitoes found us, too. My wife, never a lover of the great outdoors, was ready to leave, but not me or my son! What a beautiful location, I thought. I could hear the water as it flowed over the riffles before entering the Katie hole, and looking through the hemlock branches I could see the moon and stars. The smell of that kerosene lantern or the high pitched sound of mosquitoes around my ears didn't bother me too much. Jeff, my four year old, was asleep on his cot completely oblivious to everything that I thought was wonderful and what his mother thought was horrendous!

However, after a couple hours, the moon disappeared, no stars were visible, and the sky was brightened at times from lightning in the distance. Soon it was not distant lightning – it seemed to be right over top of us, with immediate claps of thunder. "We're getting out of here," I was told. So, I picked up my son and with my good wife following, made my way to the car—less than a quarter mile away. We drove the short distance to my parents' house and ended out first camping experience there. It was 2:00 o'clock in the morning. Oh, yes, it did rain and my wife was absolutely correct in insisting we leave when we did – being in a tent under a tall tree is not the best place to be during a thunder storm. The next day I drove to our camp site, struck my tent, carried my gear to the car – dragged my boat to the road and after a struggle loaded it onto the car top carrier and headed home. Never again did we use the open face Baker tent—nor a kerosene lantern on a camping trip. Retired, too, were the uncomfortable army cots with the cheap inflatable plastic mattresses. My wife made certain that we upgraded our camping gear before our next adventure.

This view was taken from the site of our first camping trip looking downstream from the Katie Hole.

Chapter 8

History and Geography of the Area

Brief History of Union, Mann and Southampton Township

For as long as I can remember I have had an interest in local history. The areas that I visited most and with which I was most familiar were in the southeastern part of Bedford County – Southampton and Mann Townships, and Union Township in Fulton County. Perhaps my interest was intensified by the many arrow heads and stone chips that I found and attributed to work done by Indians many, many years before white men moved into the area. The meadow below my grandparents' house was the source of many finds of arrow heads – some perfect, some broken, and pieces of flat stones that I presumed were scrapers. In later years I would learn that Pennsylvania had no permanent Indian people living within its borders, but it was home to Indians of different tribes at various periods of history. And in the geographical area about which I write, the terrain, the flora, the streams, and the many springs must have been very favorable for wild life that in turn, attracted Indian hunters to the region. As mentioned previously, the Barnes' family settlement in what would be called, Barnes's Gap, was reported to be at the site of an old Indian Camp. Incidentally, abundant wildlife was also an attraction for some of the early white settlers to the region, also.

The area about which I write did not have the same influx of settlers as was true in the north and east in Fulton County. The Scots-Irish and some German settlers had moved into the Great Cove area and the Big and Little Conolloways in relatively large numbers quite early. The Scots-Irish or Scotch – Irish as they were sometimes called, were Scots who had moved to northern Ireland and had lived there for several generations.

However, prior to their emigration from northern Ireland they were often at odds with the Irish Catholics because of religious differences – the Scots-Irish were largely Presbyterians; additionally, the land owners in northern Ireland at the time were primarily English. These land owners increasingly raised the rents on their Scots-Irish tenants to the point that they could not afford to pay. As a consequence thousands of them immigrated to Pennsylvania and other colonies. Sometimes as single families; other times an entire congregation would move led by their minister. The land on which the Scots-Irish settled in Pennsylvania – referenced above, had not been "purchased" from the Indians – nor was there any agreement with the Indians that settlers could move onto these lands. Indians were incensed that settlers were moving into areas that they considered to be their prime hunting grounds. Despite warnings from the Provincial Authorities settlers continued to move into the Great Cove and Conolloways. (Tonolloways). After Braddocks defeat in 1755, Indians, with help from the French, raided unmercifully the inhabitants of the Great Cove, The Tonolloway Settlements, and any place on the Pennsylvania Frontier where adventurous settlers had gone.

It was not until after the Revolutionary War, when the frontier was pushed farther west, that people in large numbers began moving into the areas of what are now Union, Mann, and Southampton Townships. During this time period present Fulton County was part of Bedford County. Fulton County was not established until 1850. Yes, some hardy souls were living in these areas before the Revolution, but compared to the numbers that moved in after that, the numbers were indeed small. By the 1790's danger from Indian attacks had vanished and people were moving into

Bedford County in large numbers. Many settlers in this area came by way of Virginia and Maryland. Interestingly, while many of the first settlers to this part of Pennsylvania remained and the same family names can still be found today, the wanderlust that had driven them to the new lands in Bedford County was not lost; some continued to move to new lands going south to pass through the Cumberland Gap and to form new settlements elsewhere.

The township where I lived as a boy, Union, was not formed until 1864 – (the name Union reflects the Civil War influence in the search for a name) formerly it had been a part of Bethel Township, formed in 1773 as part of Bedford County; in 1850 Bethel became a township in the newly established county of Fulton. A brief but interesting history of Union township can be found in Waterman, Watkins, and Co., *History of Bedford, Somerset and Fulton Counties*, published in 1884.

According to the account found in this publication, part of this township, now known as Buck Valley, (my home was in the southern part of the valley) was deeded to James Wilson in 1795. It changed hands a couple more times before being deeded to William Lee in 1822. The acreage was 25,000. Mr. Lee's intent was to raise sheep on the land, but ill health prevented that from happening. The 25,000 acres was eventually divided among his children and heirs. They in turn, sold it to new settlers who came into the region.

The family names of residents in Buck Valley, have always been of interest to me – so many of them are of German origin, with a sprinkling of Irish and English names. Surnames like Fischer, Sigel, Dorrier, Gienger, Shultz, Stahle, Schretrompf and others, were all familiar names of German origin in Buck Valley. If one reviews the census data of 1850 and after, it will be found that many of these settlers came from different parts of Germany. English and Irish names such as Shipway and Beatty were also among early land holders. A review of the names of Civil War and

World Wars 1 and II veterans on the Memorial at Buck Valley Park show many of these same family names.

After 1802 the United States Congress established procedures for local authorities to help grant citizenship to immigrants. Immigration data will show that the British Isles and Germany provided the largest number of new settlers to Bedford and Fulton Counties. County courthouses provide a good source for reviewing the names of immigrants as well as persons who attested to the citizenship qualities of the "would be new citizen"

Geographical Sketch of Union, Mann, and Southampton Townships

Each of the above townships lies within the Ridge and Valley physical region of the state. This region is characterized by rather steep ridges and valleys with small streams serving as miniature watersheds. The ridges generally run in a northeast to southwest direction. The eastern edge of the ridge and valley region is bordered by the Great Valley, the western edge is bounded by the Allegheny Front. Most of the ridges remain forested – for years they have provided timber for building the farm structures needed and before more convenient fuels became available for home heating, many of the trees were used as fuel for domestic purposes. Most, if not all of the forested areas today, would be of second or third generation growth.

There is a great diversity of forest growth in this region of Pennsylvania. As a boy I was interested in learning to identify the various types of vegetation that grew in areas where I would hike or fish. On our own farm the land was primarily ridge land with somewhat thin shale soil, much of it red shale. Much of my grandfather's land, however, was of a lower elevation – creek bottoms on either side of Sideling Hill Creek, where the soil was deeper and more fertile. The natural vegetation differed, too. Along the creek there were large basswood, sycamore, hickory – both shagbark and shellbark, and large sugar maple trees, plus black walnut and butternut. On the higher ridges and slopes some of the same trees might be found, but I remember many more different types of oaks, locust, black birch, wild cherry, quaking aspen, ash, and smaller under story trees such as ironwood, spicebush, June berry and red bud growing there.

On our farm after cultivation of a particular piece of land had ceased, relatively small coniferous trees, jack pines, we called them would emerge from the ground and grow in abundance. I suppose they had some value as pulp wood, but none for construction purposes. On some of the slopes that were never cultivated there were almost pure stands of yellow pines. The yellow pine and poplar provided excellent siding for many of the early barns that were built in the southeastern part of Bedford County and the southern part of Fulton County

One year when I was in the seventh or eighth grade I made a booklet with as many different leaves from our local trees as I could find. I was truly amazed at how many different types of forest vegetation grew within a ten mile radius of where I lived.

Prior to the chestnut tree blight that occurred early in the 1900's the American chestnut shared with oaks and pines as the primary trees of importance in the ridge and valley region. As a boy I remember seeing stands of dead chestnut trees – looking like so many gray ghosts on slopes of prominent ridges. These dead trees made excellent firewood. Very few, if any, can be seen today. I remember, too, seeing good size chestnut saplings attempting to make a comeback. I would check each year to see if any of them had produced a few chestnuts. They did not. After a few years the saplings would succumb to the same fungus attack that had killed the parent trees. Some of the "stake and rider" rail fences that I recall seeing on farms in my area often used the chestnut trees from which to split the rails. These types of fences made wonderful hiding places for quails and rabbits!

The demise of the American chestnut was a tremendous loss to the ridge and valley forests. It was a very valuable source of lumber – the wood had many wonderful characteristics, it was straight grained, easily worked, strong, and rot resistant. It was used for outdoor as well as indoor construction. The nuts were a prime food source for much of the wildlife of the area. Residents of the area also collected large quantities of these very edible nuts each fall.

For many years plant scientist have been working to develop a blight resistant American Chestnut tree. There is some evidence that they are succeeding. However, it is very unlikely that the forests of the ridge and valley region will ever see the return of the native American Chestnut to a degree resembling the prominence it once had.

The ridges usually run parallel to each other, accordion like, giving the appearance that they have been folded. Obviously, there is little cultivation of crops on the steep slopes – the soil is thin and infertile, but the tops of some ridges were often broad enough that cultivation could and did occur. As farming became more mechanized it was more and more confined to the valleys, often quite narrow, but relatively fertile, shale soil. Some of the early settlers did attempt to cultivate the sides of slopes – in general, wagons were not used, instead sleds with wooden runners were used to bring what scant crops were produced down from the hillsides.

Today there are fewer and fewer small family farms in operation. The trend has been for fewer farmers to cultivate greater acreage – either through purchase or rental. With the greater mechanization of farming the cultivation of larger plots of land has become a necessity.

Early settlers in this region built their homes at the base of a ridge where there would be a good, flowing spring. Nearly all the older homes in the area that I remember visiting had a spring close by – often, a shelter would be built over it and the "spring house" would serve many of the functions that the refrigerator does today

Chapter 9

Reflections

Yes, Thomas Wolfe was correct, "You can't go home again." On the preceding pages I have retraced and relived many of the experiences that occurred during childhood, and the question I asked myself is, "Would I really want to go home again?" The answer is, NO! It is interesting and emotionally satisfying to reminisce about events that occurred years ago involving very significant people who played a role in molding the kind of person I became. But the world of today is so different from that which we experienced as children that to suddenly insert ourselves into that world would be truly incompatible. I believe we tend to idealize the past, we romanticize it, we remember the positive more than the negative. Actually those "good old days" were not really that good! It is the optimism of memory, I suppose, that makes us long for the "Good Old Days".

I could not help asking questions, though, as I wrote. Questions that have no absolute answers, only conjecture and speculation! For example, I have wondered what my life would have been like had my parents not moved to that very isolated, rural farm in Pennsylvania? Suppose, I asked myself, if I had lived those formative years of childhood in metropolitan Pittsburgh where I was born? Cultural events would have been accessible, specialized lessons in art or music would have been available assuming I had the talent or inclination to pursue them, and what about the schools, certainly the menu of courses in high school would have been much more varied than was true in a rural area such as the one in which I lived? Would my parents have used the same kinds of parenting techniques with their children had they remained in an urban world? Would I have been influenced by a variety of occupations and professions that would certainly have been in evidence in a large metropolitan area as opposed to a small farming community? My answer is, well, perhaps! But, then, I wonder, would I really have developed into a different person had my physical and social environment been within an urban environment rather than a rural one? Do I believe that one's environment, inclusive of the social and physical, shapes and determines the direction of one's life? Yes, it undoubtedly exerts an influence – but how much? Regardless of where I had been reared I suspect I would have had an academic leaning. I've noted many siblings who were reared in what appeared to be the same social and physical environment often exhibits many different interests and demonstrate different behavior patterns from each other as children and as adults.

I guess I believe very strongly in heredity and, most certainly, in the nurturing influence and lasting effects that a mother has on her children in the very early months and years of life. I believe I was born with the proclivity to be an academic. My mother, knowingly or not, nurtured that tendency by reading to me from a very early age. Quite honestly, I don't believe it matters very much what the reading material is – it is the act of someone reading to the very young child that really matters. Early parental influence, I believe, is the determining factor that shapes and influences the direction that our lives take. I cannot remember any period of my life that I did not enjoy reading – and that enjoyment was never confined to any specific subject matter or topic. It has always been very eclectic. I've always been grateful to my mother and to those elementary teachers I had who placed a high value on reading – they provided me with encouragement and the necessary reading material.

I've always been a bit suspect when I hear persons blame their adult shortcomings and lack of achievements on deprivations that are associated with the social environment in which they grew up. Do not adults who perceives their own shortcomings have an obligation and responsibility to remediate them as soon as they becomes aware of them – rather than to live with the shortcomings and blame others?

I can say, with all honesty, that I'm glad I had the opportunity to live most of my boyhood as I did and where I did. Yes, my language pattern, parochial expressions, mannerisms and other tell-tale signs that speak to one's being reared in a certain locale, may have been quite evident to those who grew up in a different segment of society. But those characteristics were superficialities – the primary positive values to which I was exposed, i.e., respect for others, integrity, honesty, industry, the essence of the "Golden Rule," plus many more, were common to my community – and I believe, to many other communities all over the country during that era. And I would hope still are because they reflect, in my opinion, the essence of what it means to be a good citizen.

I am especially grateful for the fact that I was able to know so many people who lived their early lives in the last quarter of the 19th Century. Most were excellent mentors and excellent role models for me and the young kids who were my contemporaries. Added to that population would be the generation of my parents The way those two generations lived their lives gave real meaning to the sentiment, "I'd rather see a sermon than hear one."

I have no regrets of having had the experience of living through the "Great Depression". No, I wouldn't want to do it again, nor would I want to see my children or the children of anyone live through an economy such as was experienced during the 1930's. But, from the very responsible adults around me I learned about frugality and delaying gratification, – and what the real meaning is of that principle in economics that says, “Man has unlimited wants, but limited resources.” The lessons learned during that period from observing the significant people in my life have served me well in my lifetime.

I believe we have lost a sense of family during the last fifty years. Families today, because of many factors, are scattered across the country. Communication is via email, phone conversations or text messaging – letter writing has become a lost art! Children don’t really get to know their grandparents, great aunts and uncles, or for that matter, even their aunts and uncles; (some critics might even say that many children do not even get to know their parents very well – when both parents are working outside the home!) there are few opportunities where all the cousins get together to play a baseball game, hike in the woods, swim and fish – or just roughhouse with each other. (Perhaps if they did get together they would play computer games or listen to their ipods!)

I suppose my grandchildren would read the above and say, “Grandfather, you’re still living in the 20th century – everything has changed – get with it. This is the 21st century!” Perhaps they are right! But, I’m still glad I had the experiences I had during the first sixteen years of my life. Maybe fifty or sixty years from now one of them will write about his or her experiences during the early years of the 21st century. But I wonder, will the contrast between now and then be as great as the contrast that I have witnessed between the era of the 30’s and 40’s and now?

Chapter 10

Picture Gallery

Pictures and commentary of several small useful items usually found on small farms or in the home.

Mowing scythe

Corn cutter

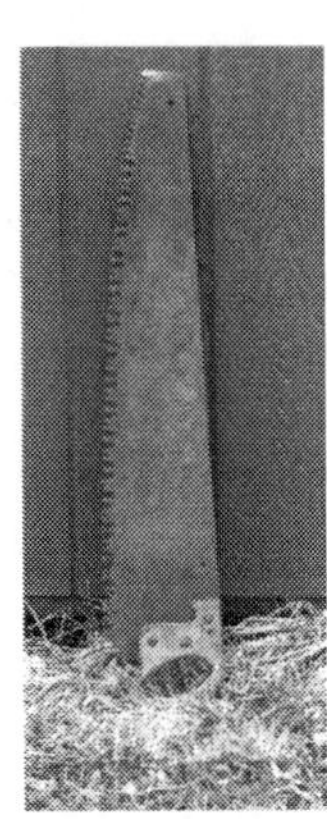
One man saw

The three items shown above were frequently used on small farms. The mowing scythe, seen on the left was often used to cut brush from fence rows, unwanted brush growing along the edge of fields, or wherever unwanted high weeds and small, woody stemmed vegetation grew. When equipped with a rather short heavy blade, my dad referred to it as a "brush hook." Road maintenance workers would use a scythe of this type when they would clear unwanted brush from road sides. This particular one was carried by me to the fields where I was supposed to cut the unwanted vegetation. The secret to efficiently using a scythe was to keep the blade very sharp by frequent application of the whetstone on the edge of the blade. My dad would say that

I didn't use the scythe enough to dull the blade! I confess, he was correct!

The second item is a corn cutter, or some persons referred to it a corn chopper. Regardless, of what it was called, it was used to cut corn stocks. Sometime during the month of September farmers in my area would sharpen the blades of their cutters and take to the cornfields. On my grandfather's farm there would be usually at least four persons who would work together – one person could work by himself, but facing a ten acre field of corn alone was a bit depressing! A "corn horse" was dragged between the rows several feet ahead of the cutters. The corn horse was nothing more than a wooden device with two front legs about thirty inches high, maybe a couple feet wide at the bottom and a ten or twelve foot two by four attached to the top of the two legs, that sloped to the ground behind the legs. Forming a rather large triangle. A hole was bored about two feet back from the front legs through which a one inch dowel, we used a broom stick handle was pushed through so that the cut corn stocks could be leaned against it from both sides. When the shock had been formed and tied at the top, the broom stick was removed and the corn horse was moved forward to be used for the next shock. This continued until all the corn was cut and shocked.

The third item shown is a one man cross cut saw. There is a hole drilled on the small end of the saw so that a handle—perpendicular to the saw could be attached if the saw were used by two sawyers. Typically, it was used by only one person to saw firewood into appropriate lengths.

My dad and I used a "two man" saw – somewhat longer than the one shown. We didn't make a very good team, though. My arms were longer than his and apparently our rhythm was off when we were pulling the saw to and fro! He'd become a bit angry at me and accused me of "riding the saw" as he put it. I wasn't – maybe it seemed that way to him because of my longer reach and different rhythm pattern in pulling the saw! I was always thankful that most of our firewood was cut into lengths by a circular saw that was belt driven with power from a tractor.

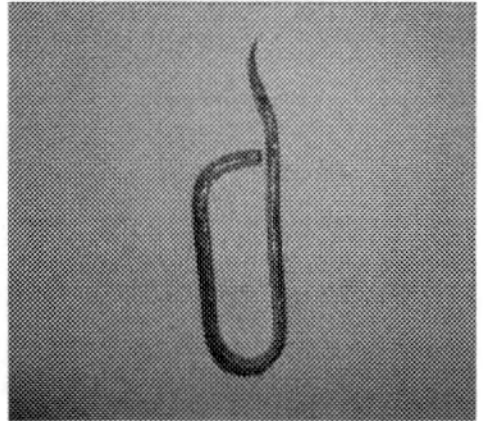 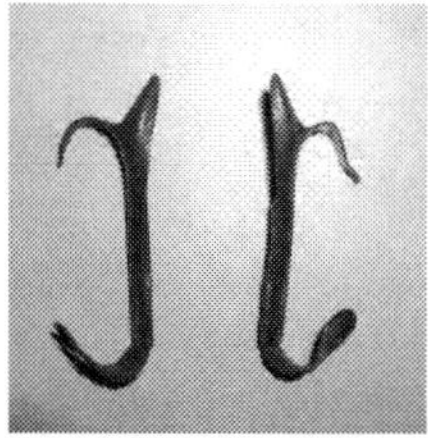 

Husking pegs

The items above show three different types of husking pegs. Husking pegs were used to remove the husks from the ears of corn. Sometimes corn was husked in the field where the corn shocks stood. Other times the corn shocks were hauled to the barn floor and husked during the winter when the weather outside was inclement. I remember being especially pleased when I would pull back the husk to discover a red ear of corn! There were different types of husking pegs. Only three different ones are shown above.

The husking peg on the left was made by my great, grandfather – he had a small shop and a small forge and an anvil – he was able to make many of the small implements needed for use on the farm. The two husking pegs in the center were of a different type. Both were made of metal; one for a left hander the other for a right handed person. The one on the left belonged to my father – he was left-handed.

The two shown on the extreme right were made with a combination of metal and leather. The top one had space for all the fingers, without any leather separating them, the bottom one separated the fingers with leather.

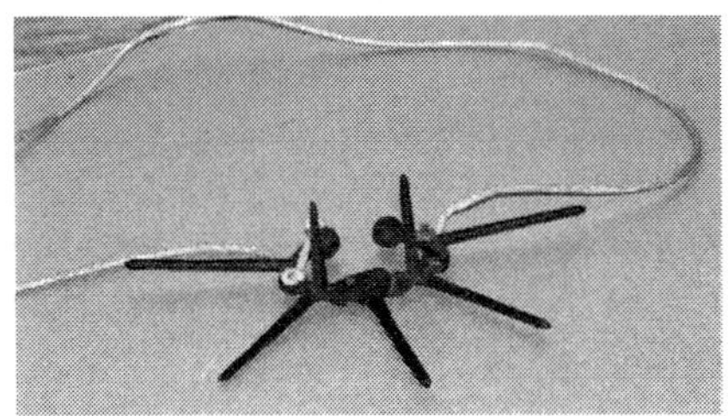

Calf Weaning Devices

The above weaning devices were placed on calves to discourage nursing when they were in the field with their mother. The devices were fitted over a calf's head in such a way that the calf could graze, but not nurse. The one on the left was held in place by two adjustable balls that fitted into the nostrils of the calf. The other one was adjusted to fit in such a way that the calf could not nurse without annoying its mother with those projections on the front of it. With either device the mother did not like the feel of the weaning device against her udder! She'd walk away from her calf.

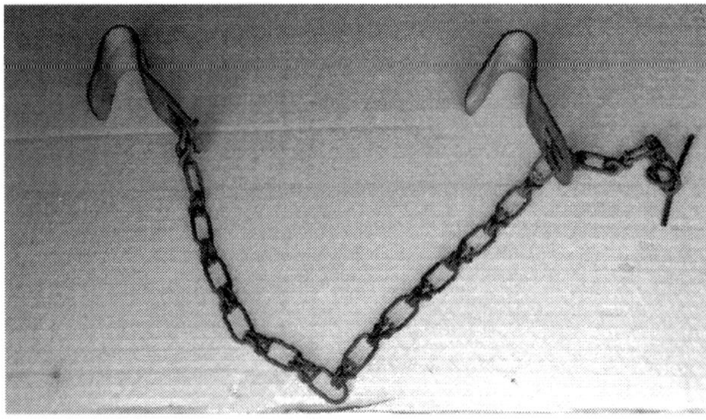

Cow Kickers

Some cows had a tendency to kick when being milked. Maybe they objected to those cold hands in the early morning; whatever the reason rather than having the bucket of milk upset by a swift kick from her, the farmer might put a set of kickers on the hind legs of the cow. The kickers could be adjusted so that her hind legs were closer or farther apart. Rather than go to the trouble of putting on those kickers I preferred putting my head in the flank of the cow. This prevented her from kicking so freely. And, I was able to feel the beginning motion of the kick to come – thus, I was able to move the bucket before she upset it, or what was worse, set her foot in the bucket!

Singletree

The singletree would have been found on any farm that used horses. In the picture above, the item to be pulled by the horse – cart, sled, plow, etc. would have been attached to the ring seen at the end of the chain in the foreground. Trace chains attached to the hames – which rests against the collar around the neck of the horse, (all part of the harness) were connected to both sides of the singletree.

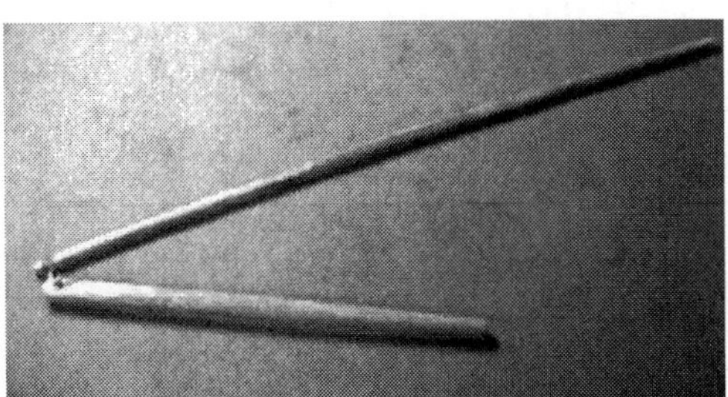

Flail

This pioneer farm implement was found in an old barn in Fulton County. The flail was widely used for threshing grain before the threshing machine came into common use. The shorter end was attached to the longer shaft by a leather thong. It was made to swivel around the shaft as the farmer beat the wheat, or whatever grain crop had been placed on the barn floor. The beating process shook the grain from the plant heads. The next step in the threshing process was to place the straw and chaff into a basket, take it outside on a windy day, and toss it into the air. The wind would blow the chaff and straw away and the heavier grain would fall to the ground to be swept up by the farmer.

Small battery flashlight and three kerosene barn lanterns

Outdoor Lighting on Our Farm

During the 1930's and 1940's many small farms were without electricity. Early morning and after dark outside chores meant lighting the kerosene barn lantern. The three lanterns seen in the picture above were all Dietz barn lanterns. By the 1930's and 1940's many of the earlier makers of kerosene lanterns had gone out of business or had been bought out by Dietz. Lanterns usually had names – the one on the extreme right was named "Wizard with Large Fount," it would burn for several hours on one filling. Next, on the left, is a smaller lantern called the "Little Wizard". Each of these two lanterns was known as a "Cold blast" lantern. In a cold blast type lantern the cold, fresh air was drawn into the tubes directly below the top of the lantern and fed to the flame from under the burner. This type barn lantern burned with a brighter flame, with less flicker than was true of the next lantern seen in the picture on the left of the two previously discussed. This Dietz lantern, a "Hot Blast" type, was named, Royal. In a hot blast type some of the warm, exhaust air rising above the flame is drawn back down the tubes and fed through the burner to the flaming wick again. The flame is somewhat less bright than that provided by a cold blast lantern. The hot blast lantern was also more subject to being affected by winds and strong drafts. We had both types at our house. As a boy I was not aware of the function of the side tubes on lanterns; I did not realize that the tubes actually provided oxygen to the flame! I carried a "Little Wizard" lantern to the barn each school morning during the winter month when I would milk the cows. A lantern at my parents' home was not used in the barn in the evening – the barn work was done before it got dark. However, there were other uses for it. An unexpected emergency trip to the "outhouse" often required a lighted lantern to light that "path to the bathroom"! And, anyone who ever fished at night during the 1930's or 1940's would no doubt have taken along a smelly, rusted kerosene lantern!

The little battery-operated flashlight seen on the extreme right is like one I had during the early 1940's. It was powered by two D cells batteries. It was called the "Niagara Junior Guide" and was advertised as being so powerful that it, "Bores a 300 Foot Hole in the Night." I don't believe I ever tried to verify that claim but I did use that little flashlight for many years.

Four Kerosene Lamps

Home Lighting in Many Farm Homes

The four lamps shown above were typical of the types used during the 1930's and early 1940's in many rural farming communities in Pennsylvania. The lamp on the extreme right is an Aladdin lamp, by far the brightest of all kerosene lamps used in a farm home. It differed from other kerosene lamps in that its bright light was produccd by a mantle that glowed to incandesces when heated by a lighted circular wick. The mantle was treated with rare earth materials – it was very fragile and easily damaged. The light produced by an Aladdin lamp was a bright, white light that resembled very closely the light from an electric light bulb. I believe its light was approximately rated as 60 candle power. The lamp produced a great deal of heat; care had to be taken that the top of the lamp chimney was not too close to any combustible material. It also consumed a great deal of oxygen in a room good ventilation was recommended if used in a small room. Shades were recommended for Aladdin lamps because of the brightness of the glowing mantle.

The lamp shown to the left of the Aladdin was sold as a kitchen lamp, although many were used elsewhere in the home. It, too, used a circular burner and wick, but had no mantle. Instead its light was produced by the flaming wick. It was somewhat brighter than the other two kerosene lamps shown, but only because the surface area of the flaming wick was larger. Many of these lamps were used – when used on a table the shade tended to reflect the light downward; making it quite suitable to read by.

The lamp to the left of the shaded lamp was a very common kerosene lamp, probably made in the 1920's or 30's and sold by most general stores of that era. I read many books and did my home work with the light of this particular lamp. My mother laughed when I showed her the "spliced" wick – a piece of cotton had been attached to the store bought wick. She said, "You can call that a Depression wick; I attached a piece of cotton to the wick so I wouldn't have to buy a new one!" Even with a freshly washed globe, a neatly trimmed wick, and a font full of fresh kerosene, the light was not very bright – it had a distinct, yellowish cast to it. As the wick charred somewhat, because of the build up of carbon on its surface, and the globe became darkened from carbon (this would happen if the flame was too high – it would smoke) the amount of light was reduced considerably. We had several such lamps – upstairs and downstairs.

The last lamp – on the extreme left, was a small hand lamp or sometimes called a finger lamp. My grandmother had owned this particular one; the pattern was called the Coolidge pattern, so named because a lamp with this pattern was found in the home of Calvin Coolidge at the time of his death.

Because of their relatively small size they were easily carried up and down stairs and were often used in the bedrooms. However, because of the small burner and small wick size the light produced was not very great.

Family Pictures

Our parents' 50th wedding anniversary
Back row – Agnes, Jerri, Alta –
Front row—Bill, Dad, Mom, Leon

Dad ready for work

Dad and his new Kaiser

Alta and I ride a pony

Mom on the steps

Siblings – Agnes, Alta and Jerri

Audy Northcraft, Jerri, and Agnes
waiting to help me unload the wagon.

Mom her baby (me) and my oldest sister, Alta

Fifty years after it was issued I could still wear it!

Mother, and her two sisters, Zoe and Delphine Northcraft

My little brother with his big catch.

Made in the USA
Middletown, DE
27 April 2020